Propeller Handbook

Propeller Handbook

*The Complete Reference for Choosing,
Installing, and Understanding Boat Propellers*

DAVE GERR

International Marine Publishing Company
Camden, Maine

Published by International Marine Publishing Company

10 9 8 7 6 5 4 3 2 1

Copyright © 1989 International Marine Publishing Company

Library of Congress Cataloging in Publication Data

Gerr, Dave.
    Propeller handbook : the complete reference for choosing,
installing, and understanding boat propellers / Dave Gerr.
        p. cm.
    Bibliography: p.
    Includes index.
    ISBN 0-87742-988-X :
    1. Propellers. 2. Motorboats—Maintenance and re-
pair. I. Title.
VM753.G47   1989
623.8′73—dc19   89-2042
                                                                              CIP

International Marine Publishing Company offers software for sale. For
information and a catalog, please contact TAB Software Department,
Blue Ridge Summit, PA 17294-0850.

Questions regarding the content of this book should be
addressed to:

International Marine Publishing Company
Division of TAB Books, Inc.
P.O. Box 220
Camden, ME 04843

Typeset by Graphic Composition, Athens, GA
Printed by Alpine Press, Stoughton, MA
Design by Abby Trudeau
Production by Janet Robbins
Edited by Jonathan Eaton and David Oppenheim
Cover photo courtesy W. H. Den Ouden Vetus (U.S.A.) Inc.

To my father and my mother,
without whom this book could
not have been written.

Contents

Formula Contents _____

Table Contents

Chart Contents ──

Acknowledgments ─────────────────────────────────

The author wishes to express his thanks to the many individuals and companies who generously provided assistance and advice. A few who require special note are:

Spyros N. Garbis, who has been a source of guidance and encouragement for many years. Ted Brewer and Joe Peterson, both of whom pointed out a few errors before it was too late. Caterpillar Inc., The Cummins Engine Company, Inc., and The Michigan Wheel Corporation, all of whom went out of their way to provide much needed information. My editor, Jonathan Eaton, whose advice and patience has been much appreciated. And the *real* propeller experts—the many, many researchers and engineers, from Admiral David Taylor to the present day—who painstakingly and expertly gathered the fundamental information without which this book could not have been written.

Introduction: *Using This Book* ─────────────────────

This book is not for Ph.D.s seeking the latest wrinkle in high-tech propeller design. Rather, it's for the average mechanic, engineer, fleet operator, port captain, serious yachtsman, and naval architect as a clear and easy-to-use reference for choosing the correct propeller for a particular design and service.

It is necessary to take the time to make sense of a few tables and graphs; however, all the calculations can be done by anyone with a basic understanding of high-school math. In fact, every formula presented here can be solved readily using the simplest and least expensive scientific calculators. (Appendix D presents a quick refresher course in using decimal exponents.)

One of the more puzzling concepts in propeller selection is the degree of accuracy that is either desirable or attainable. A reference containing detailed charts, tables, and formulas seems to call for extreme accuracy. Actually, all propeller selection is a process of approximation and estimation. It is important that you avoid mathematical errors when solving the formulas required or when reading values from a graph or table, but the degree of real-world accuracy you can achieve is limited.

There are two reasons for this. The first is that the interactions of the water, propeller, and hull with each other are so complex that no one really understands exactly what is happening. Even for a very straightforward installation, an engineer would have to be able to predict not only exactly how the water flow behaves as it swirls through the propeller blades, but how the shape of the hull affects that flow. Then, this engineer would have to determine precisely how these factors change—and they can change a great deal—at different speeds, loadings, and sea states. And this is just the tip of the iceberg. Shaft angle, boat trim, rudder angle, stern gear, exhaust back pressure, water temperature, and so on all play significant roles in propeller performance and behavior.

The second reason that propeller selection remains an approximate undertaking is that for almost every ordinary vessel you will be selecting from the available stock commercial propellers. The variety of these propellers is more than wide enough to meet the needs of almost any application; however, it is nearly impossible to account for the many subtle differences between similar propellers of different manufacture.

A manufacturer of folding sailboat propellers recently ran a test series against similar propellers of other manufacturers. They found that, even after carefully selecting similar propellers, propellers of nominally identical face pitch actually measured significantly different pitches. When the radical differences in blade style, camber, and thickness were considered it became nearly impossible to find any two propellers that were really identical in measurements, even though many had a catalog specification of the same diameter and pitch. The selection of folding sailboat propellers is limited, so this is a somewhat extreme example; nevertheless, you can specify a commercial propeller only within reasonable limits. Diameter, face pitch, blade thickness, disk area ratio, and several additional factors serve to pin the design down fairly well, yet leave room for noticeable differences among propellers of varying style and manufacture.

It is thus important, when selecting a propeller, not to let yourself get bogged down in a pursuit of extreme numerical accuracy. Engineers use the term "significant digits" to indicate the degree of accuracy possible with a given amount of data. Computer programmers use the earthier "garbage in, garbage out." This simply means that your answer can never be more accurate than the information you started with.

For the vast majority of applications, simply working through the procedures in this book will enable you to select a propeller that will perform admirably. For uses in which

─────────────────────

extreme accuracy is required—squeezing the top one-half of one percent in performance from a racing boat or obtaining the nth degree of maximum fuel economy in a tug fleet—additional investigation may be justified. In such cases tank testing and detailed computer analysis may be called for, but ultimately the final decision will be made by running the vessel over a measured course with a number of differing propellers and carefully evaluating the results. Except for such unusual and exacting installations, using this handbook and testing an array of the most promising stock propellers will give results equal to any other method known.

Factors in Propeller Selection

A common misconception in selecting a propeller is that it is only necessary to specify diameter and pitch. Although these factors are the most critical—as mentioned earlier—there are many other characteristics that must be considered. If, for instance, you simply want a propeller 24 inches in diameter and with a 20-inch pitch, on opening the manufacturer's catalog you would discover eight or nine very different types of propellers available in these dimensions. Which should you choose? Among other things, you have to consider the number of blades, blade area, blade thickness, section shape, and so on. All of these characteristics are dealt with in detail in Chapter 4.

Understanding how blade shape, area, and configuration affect performance will enable you not only to specify general propeller dimensions, but to specify the most suitable propeller type and pattern as well. Attempting to select a propeller on the basis of pitch and diameter alone is like walking into a hardware store and asking simply for a 3/4-inch, number 8 screw. The shopkeeper would immediately ask you if you need a wood screw, sheet metal screw, or a machine screw; a phillips-head or standard slot; a round head, oval, or flat; one made of bronze or steel; and so on. Purchasing a 3/4-inch number 8 machine screw for a woodworking project would be nearly useless. It is equally important to specify the correct type of propeller.

Before you can properly specify and order the most suitable propeller for your application, you must specify most of the following factors, listed roughly in order of importance:

1 Diameter
2 Pitch
3 Number of blades
4 Hand (left- or right-hand turning)
5 Propeller shaft diameter and keyway
6 Blade area (usually using Mean-Width Ratio or Disc-Area Ratio)
7 Cupped or uncupped blades
8 Supercavitating or standard noncavitating blades
9 Blade section shape (airfoil, ogival or combined)
10 Skew
11 Rake
12 Blade thickness
13 Hub diameter

Items 1 through 6 must be specified for every propeller and every installation. Items 7 through 13 are of greater importance for differing types of craft and in solving specific problems. Skewed blades, for instance, might be indicated where vibration is a problem;

supercavitating blades are only called for on very high-speed craft; and thick blades would be specified on low-speed workboats operating in waters littered with debris.

Plan of This Book

It is the intent of this handbook to provide all the basic information required to select propellers for almost every ordinary type of boat, from a sailing auxiliary, to a high-speed powerboat, to a trawler, and so on. If you are interested in one particular type of vessel or application, it is not necessary to study every section of every chapter. The best approach is to skim through the entire book, then concentrate on the sections that apply to your application.

Chapters 1 and 2 cover questions in determining speed and power.

Chapter 3 describes the basic parts and dimensions of a propeller.

Chapter 4 discusses and defines the differences in blade shape and propeller type.

Chapter 5 covers the simpler "slip method" of propeller selection, best suited to pleasure craft, and most notably to sailing auxiliaries.

Chapter 6 details the mathematically more exact BP-δ method of propeller selection.

Chapter 7 answers questions regarding installations, such as blade clearances, propeller shafting, etc.

Chapters 8 and 9 discuss some special considerations required for tugs, trawlers, sailboats and high-speed and outboard-powered yachts.

Chapter 1
Power

Understanding Engine Performance

A propeller must satisfy two basic requirements. It needs to match the engine's power and shaft speed, and it must match the size and operating speed of the boat. But the size of the engine affects boat speed, and the type of hull affects the choice of engine. This circular relationship, with one factor affecting another, which in turn affects the first factor, is inescapable in propeller selection.

These basic requirements engender some of the most frequently asked questions about propellers: Why won't my engine reach its top rated RPM? Will more or less pitch improve my boat's performance? Why doesn't my boat reach the top speed claimed by the manufacturer? Before we can answer these and other such questions, we have to investigate power, engine performance, and speed in some detail.

Obviously, the more power available (all other things being equal), the faster a boat will go. Accordingly, one of the very first decisions that must be made in selecting an engine and propeller, whether for repowering, for a new design, or simply to improve performance, is the speed of operation desired.

Using the tables and methods in Chapter 2, you can calculate the speed that a vessel will make with a given power. From there, knowing both speed and power, you will have two of the basic factors needed to choose a suitable propeller, using the methods in Chapters 5 and 6. Before we can jump ahead to estimating speed, however, we have to understand what power is and how it relates to torque and fuel consumption. There are, in fact, a number of different classifications or types of power relating to marine engines.

MEASURES OF POWER

In the English system, one *horsepower* (HP) equals 33,000 foot-pounds of work per minute, or 550 foot-pounds of work per second, a foot-pound being the work expended to lift a weight of one pound through a distance of one foot. One horsepower also equals 0.7457 *kilowatt,* which is the metric measure of power. One kilowatt equals 1000 joules per second, or 1000 newton-meters per second. There is also a metric horsepower (HK or PK), which is equal to 0.9863 English-measure HP.

Effective Horsepower, EHP

Effective horsepower or *EHP* is the power required to overcome a vessel's resistance at a given speed, not including the power required to turn her own propeller and operate her machinery. This is very close to the amount of power required to tow the vessel.

Indicated Horsepower, IHP

Indicated horsepower or *IHP* is the power required to drive the vessel at a given speed. Indicated horsepower includes the power needed to overcome friction in machinery and to turn the propeller through the water. The ratio of EHP/IHP is usually around 50 percent; in other words, the indicated horsepower is usually about twice the effective horsepower, but this will vary with the installation. Neither EHP nor IHP can be determined without access to sophisticated tank test results or computer prediction programs, and neither figures in the propeller selection methods of this book.

Brake Horsepower, BHP

The *brake horsepower* or *BHP* of an engine is the maximum horsepower generated by the engine at a given RPM, as tested by the manufacturer. It is important to know whether the BHP has been measured with or without a reduction or reverse gear installed. (The reduction gear steps down the engine RPM to a lower shaft RPM, and the reverse gear reverses the direction of shaft and propeller rotation. In the great majority of small-boat installations, the reverse and reduction gears are combined in the same housing.) *Maximum brake horsepower* is the maximum power delivered by an engine, almost always at its maximum attainable RPM.

In common usage, brake horsepower, when used without an indication of RPM, is taken to mean maximum brake horsepower. Brake horsepower should be somewhat greater than indicated horsepower to allow for the power required by generators, compressors, and other machinery driven by the engine and not directly used to propel the vessel.

Shaft Horsepower, SHP

Shaft horsepower or *SHP* is the power actually transmitted along the propeller shaft to the propeller at a given RPM. Shaft horsepower is the brake horsepower minus the power used by all internal machinery; the power lost in the gearbox, about 3 percent (if not already deducted in the brake horsepower); and the power lost to the friction of shaft bearings, about 1½ percent per bearing. *Maximum shaft horsepower* is the maximum power delivered to the propeller, almost always at maximum attainable RPM.

It is important to remember that SHP is the measure that should actually be used in making propeller calculations. In the absence of detailed information, maximum SHP may be assumed to be 96 percent of maximum BHP. Like brake horsepower, the term shaft horsepower, when used without an indication of RPM, is taken to mean maximum shaft horsepower.

Effects of Horsepower

Obviously, more power permits more work to be done in a given time. This means that an increase in horsepower in a given hull permits either an increase in speed or an increase in the load that may be towed. Too little power will not drive a vessel at the desired speed, while too much will be wasteful of fuel, space, and initial expense.

Power and Energy Losses

It is interesting to see approximately where the energy from the fuel goes. About 35 percent is lost in heat to the atmosphere, 25 percent is lost in heat and vibration to the water, and 2 percent is lost at the propeller shaft. This leaves only about 38 percent of the energy in the fuel for propulsion. Of this 38 percent, as a very rough guide, about 3 percent is used to overcome air resistance, 27 percent to overcome wave resistance, 17 percent to overcome resistance from the wake and propeller wash against the hull; 18 percent to overcome skin friction; and 35 percent to turn the propeller. These are average values only; actual values will vary greatly from one type of boat to the next.

TORQUE (T)

In order for horsepower to propel a boat it must be converted to a twisting force rotating the propeller. This twisting force is called *torque*. In the English system, torque is a force in pounds times a distance in feet. Picture a weight of 100 pounds applied to the end of a 10-foot lever that pivots about its other end. The resultant torque is 1,000 pound-feet. In the metric system, force is measured in newtons, n, or kilograms of force, kgf, and distance in meters, m. By convention, engineers refer to torque as pound-feet, newton-meters, or kilogram-meters.

In the English system, foot-pounds really means exactly the same thing as pound-feet; however—again, by convention—this term is properly reserved for describing work, and not the torque of rotating systems. Many engineers and references are sloppy about this convention, so you should be prepared to interpret foot-pounds as torque when appropriate.

For internal combustion engines *torque,* by long-accepted definition, is 5,252 times horsepower divided by RPM. Thus, the lower the RPM and the higher the HP, the greater the torque. This is why slower-turning propellers deliver more thrust—they are receiving more torque for the same HP. For example, an engine delivering 500 HP at 2,000 RPMs would be delivering 1,313 pound-feet of torque to the propeller. If a 3:1 reduction gear were installed, SHP would be reduced approximately 3 percent by frictional losses in the reduction gear to 485 HP. At the same time, though, the shaft RPM would drop to 667, causing the torque delivered to increase to 3,819 pound-feet.

Formula 1-1   Torque Formula

Torque = T
T = (5,252 × HP) ÷ RPM
Where:
HP = horsepower (English measure)
RPM = revolutions per minute

Formula 1-1

ENGINE PERFORMANCE CURVES

The power and torque available from an engine are clearly defined by that engine's performance curves. These curves are available on performance curve sheets, distributed by most manufacturers, that plot BHP, torque, and fuel consumption against RPM. A few manufacturers include the curve of SHP, which will fall just under the BHP curve. Such SHP curves deduct power lost in the gearbox (also known as the transmission, of course) but do not include deductions for shaft bearings after the gearbox or for power used by auxiliary equipment. These power losses must still be deducted where applicable to obtain true SHP at the propeller, using 1½ percent for the power loss at each bearing and the rated horsepower of auxiliary generators, refrigeration units, hydraulic motors, etc.

Propeller Power and Fuel Consumption Curves

Two additional curves are sometimes included on the performance curve sheet. One is the theoretical propeller power curve and the other is the propeller fuel consumption curve.

The theoretical propeller power curve is an approximate representation of an average propeller's power requirements at various RPMs. For most fixed-pitch propellers that match their engines correctly, the propeller power curve crosses the shaft horsepower curve near the maximum RPM and maximum SHP. This means that when the engine is turning at top RPM, it will—in theory—be delivering exactly the power required by the propeller. (Intuition tells us that the propeller power curve is related to the indicated horsepower, IHP, but the relationship is not simple and not particularly relevant to the purposes of this book.)

The theoretical propeller power curve is taken from the formula:

Formula 1-2   Propeller Horsepower Curve Formula

Formula 1-2

$$PHP = C_{sm} \times RPM^n$$

Where:

C_{sm} = sum matching constant

n = exponent from 2.2 to 3.0, with 2.7 being used for average boats

RPM = revolutions per minute

The sum matching constant, in this case, is arbitrarily chosen to make the propeller power curve cross the SHP curve at maximum RPM. In fact, much of the process of propeller selection detailed in Chapters 5 and 6 is—in effect—determining this value exactly. Choosing the correct propeller pitch, diameter, and blade area will ensure that

Figure 1-1

Typical performance curve sheet for a small marine diesel engine. The topmost curve (1) is the brake horsepower curve. The dotted curve (2) below is the shaft horsepower curve, which shows the power delivered to the shaft just abaft the reverse/reduction gear. The dotted curve in the middle (3) is a typical propeller power curve, in this case based on the 2.7 exponent. Curve 4 is the fuel consumption curve for both brake and shaft horsepower (or the curve of specific fuel consumption), and curve 5 is the propeller fuel consumption curve.

(Courtesy of Cummins Engine Company, Inc.)

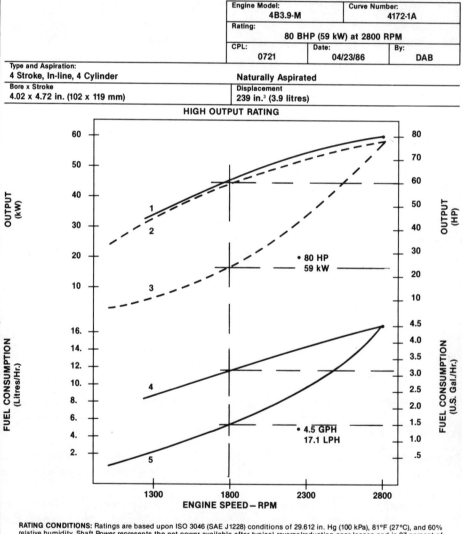

Engine Model:		Curve Number:	
4B3.9-M		**4172-1A**	
Rating:			
80 BHP (59 kW) at 2800 RPM			
CPL:	Date:		By:
0721	**04/23/86**		**DAB**

Type and Aspiration:
4 Stroke, In-line, 4 Cylinder   **Naturally Aspirated**

Bore x Stroke
4.02 x 4.72 in. (102 x 119 mm)   Displacement   **239 in.³ (3.9 litres)**

HIGH OUTPUT RATING

RATING CONDITIONS: Ratings are based upon ISO 3046 (SAE J1228) conditions of 29.612 in. Hg (100 kPa), 81°F (27°C), and 60% relative humidity. Shaft Power represents the net power available after typical reverse/reduction gear losses and is 97 percent of rated power. Fuel consumption is based upon No. 2 diesel fuel with a fuel weight of 7.1 lbs. per U.S. gal. (0.85 kg/litre) and the power requirements of a typical fixed pitch propeller.

1. Brake Horsepower (BHP).   4. Fuel Consumption for Brake and Shaft Horsepower.
2. Shaft Horsepower (SHP) with Reverse Reduction Gear.   5. Fuel Consumption for Typical Propeller.
3. Typical Propeller Power Curve (2.7 exponent).

HIGH OUTPUT RATING: This power rating is for use in variable load applications where full power is limited to two hours out of every six hours of operation. Reduced power operation must be at least 200 RPM below rated RPM. This rating is an ISO fuel stop power rating (ISO 3046), and is for applications that operate less than 600 hours per year.

the power requirements of the propeller match the engine correctly. The propeller power curve on the engine performance sheets, however, is only theoretical. It is a good approximation, useful for visualizing the relationship between specific engines and propeller power.

The exponent, n, has been found by experience to be 2.7 for almost all medium- to high-speed pleasure vessels, passenger vessels, and light commercial vessels. Heavy commercial craft operating at low speed usually have high-thrust and high-pitch-ratio propellers. For such propellers, n should be taken as 3.0. At the other end of the spectrum, ducted propellers, due to decreases in radial power losses, are best described with an n of 2.2.

Propeller power curves are a useful adjunct but are not central to the selection methods discussed in Chapters 5 and 6.

RELATIONSHIP OF ENGINE POWER TO PROPELLER POWER

One of the basic problems in selecting a standard fixed-pitch propeller is apparent in Figure 1-1. The BHP and SHP curves are shaped very differently from the propeller power curve. You can get them to match at one point—the point where they cross—but they will not match at more than this one point. Since the engine must be free to reach its maximum RPM—or very close to it—you have no choice but to select a propeller that matches the engine power at close to the top RPM as well.

If you were to choose a propeller that crossed the SHP curve at well under full RPM—curve A in Figure 1-2—the engine would be be overloaded at any higher speed. It would never reach its full RPM, and if the RPMs are held too low the engine will smoke and foul its valves. A propeller power curve like curve A indicates excessive propeller pitch, excessive propeller diameter, or both. On the other hand, if the propeller selected had such low power requirements that it never crossed the SHP curve—curve B in Figure 1-2—the full power of the engine would never be used. Such a propeller would spin inef-

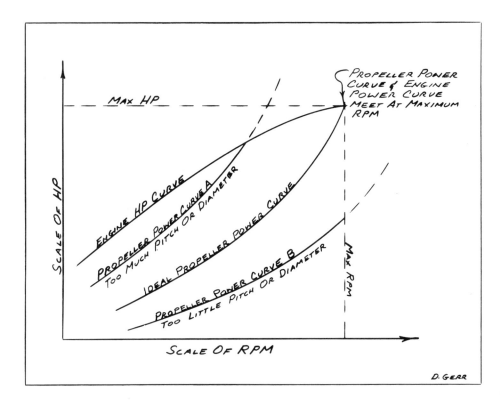

Figure 1-2

Engine and propeller power curves.

fectually and produce little thrust—an indication of too little pitch and/or too little diameter. In extreme cases, such a propeller could allow your engine to race over its top rated RPM and destroy itself.

Here we have given the basic answer to the question, "Why won't my engine reach its top RPM?" The propeller has too much diameter or too much pitch for the engine, and switching to a propeller with less diameter, pitch, or both would allow the engine to turn up to speed. You should not be too quick to rush out and change the propeller for this reason alone, however. Many engine manufacturers give the maximum rated power of their engines at the maximum RPM attainable in ideal conditions. As we will see later, it is often a good idea to size the propeller to cross the engine power curve a bit below top rated RPM. If your engine is reaching 95 percent or more of its top RPM, the propeller is probably sized quite well. If you are unable to reach 90 to 95 percent of the top RPM, there is reason to be concerned.

Effect of Low Propeller Power at Slow RPMs

In Figure 1-1 you can see that the SHP at 1,800 RPMs is about 60 (45 kw). At the same time, the propeller is using only about 22 HP (16.4 kw). Where did the missing 38 HP (28.3 kw) go? The answer is that the engine is not generating it. (The SHP curve shows potential, not actual, output.) When you adjust the throttle of a marine engine, you are not directly adjusting fuel flow to the engine. Instead, you are adjusting a governor that regulates fuel flow to maintain a constant RPM—not unlike the cruise control on a car. Since the propeller only requires 22 HP at 1,800 RPMs, the governor limits fuel flow to the engine, reducing the power generated at this RPM and—not incidentally—the fuel consumption. This lower fuel consumption is reflected in curve 5 in Figure 1-1, the propeller fuel consumption curve. At this lower RPM, additional machinery may be run off the engine without reducing RPM or slowing the vessel, although fuel consumption increases. As RPMs increase, however, the reserve or unused power decreases.

Figure 1-3

Performance curves of another engine, showing torque and fuel consumption.

(Courtesy of J.H. Westerbeke Corp.)

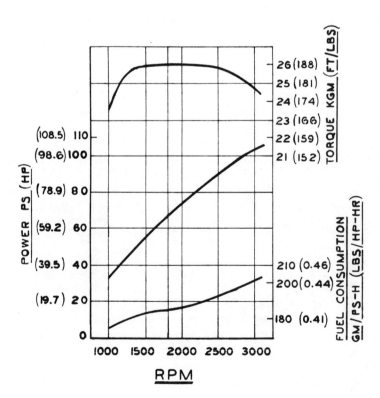

The Torque Curve

Figure 1–3 shows the performance curves of another engine. This manufacturer has plotted the torque and fuel consumption but omitted the theoretical propeller curves.

It is important to note that the maximum torque of most engines occurs below maximum RPM. This presents yet another conflict for propeller selection. Although the propeller must be chosen so that the engine can approach very close to its top rated RPM, the RPM at maximum torque frequently is as low as 50 percent of top RPM on light, high-speed engines. The only thing to do is compromise, and in so doing take fuel consumption and engine longevity into consideration as well. Specific fuel consumption is usually lowest at around 70 percent of top RPM, and torque at this RPM is still fairly high. For this reason, the most economical and efficient speed of operation of many engines (particularly light, high-speed engines) is around 70 to 85 percent of the top rated RPM, and it is usually wise to choose an engine powerful enough to push the boat at cruising speed at this reduced RPM.

Then a propeller must be chosen that will absorb the engine's power output as efficiently as possible at 70 to 85 percent of top rated RPM while still allowing the engine, when necessary or desirable, to reach its maximum rated speed.

Keep in mind that the most economical operating speed varies with the engine. The exact RPM that delivers the best combination of high torque, low fuel consumption, and longevity can be found on the engine's performance curves and by discussing your needs and intended use with the manufacturer.

Duty Rating and Operating RPM

Marine engines are manufactured in a number of *duty* or *power ratings*. These ratings determine whether the engine is intended for continuous or only short-term operation at maximum RPM. Table 1-1 gives recommended continuous operating RPMs as a percent of top rated RPM for various duty ratings.

TABLE 1-1   Recommended RPM for Continuous Operation

Type of Engine	% of max RPM
Light-duty gasoline and diesel automotive conversions	70–80%
Light-duty or high-output marine diesels	80–85%
Intermittent-duty marine diesels	88–92%
Continuous-duty heavy marine diesels	98–100%

TABLE 1-1

Continuous-duty marine engines can operate indefinitely at their top RPMs, but there is a penalty: They must be "detuned" to operate at lower top RPMs, which increases reliability and engine life but also decreases maximum horsepower and increases engine weight and cost per horsepower delivered. Intermittent-duty marine engines are intended for operation at around 90 percent or more of top RPM for no more than six hours out of every twelve. They are a good choice for many workboats. Light-duty or high-output engines should not be operated at top RPM for more than two hours in every six of operation or for more than 500 hours per year; the remainder of the time they should be operated at 80 to 85 percent of top RPM. Because of their high power output for the weight and cost, light-duty engines and light-duty automotive conversions (engines not specifically developed for marine and industrial work) are used in most yachts and small commercial vessels under 40 to 45 feet.

As a practical matter, even continuous- and intermittent-duty engines should be selected so that they operate most of the time between 80 and 90 percent of top RPM. If such engines must be run at over 90 percent of top RPM to make average cruising speed, there will be very little reserve power for special conditions—heavy weather, unusual loading, and so on. On the other hand, if they are run for long periods at well under 80 percent of top RPM, engine fouling will result.

Chapter 2
Estimating Speed
Effects of Power, Weight, and Hull Type

Now that we have examined power and engine performance, we can determine what size engine to choose for a desired speed or load with a given hull.

Engine power must continually overcome the resistance of water and air—forces that are trying to slow and stop the boat. If we could figure the exact resistance for the craft in question at the speed desired, we could choose an engine and propeller combination that generates this much thrust and thus drives the vessel at speed.

Unfortunately, determining an actual figure for resistance—a precise number of pounds—is a fantastically laborious and time-consuming task. Any sort of accuracy requires extensive tank testing and detailed computer analysis of the results, and even then there is room for considerable error. For instance, it is rare for vessels to float on their originally designed lines. Even if a vessel starts out smack on its intended waterline, the addition of new gear is likely to set it down by several inches and put it somewhat out of trim by the bow or stern. Very small differences in trim and loading can significantly affect computer and tank test resistance predictions.

Of course, the original tank testing and computer analysis can be extended to cover varying trim and load conditions, but this makes the process even more expensive. Even worse, with all the advances we have made, there are still many unknowns involved in allowing for scale effects, especially with regard to such things as the point of change from laminar (smooth) to turbulent flow.

The cost of tank testing and computer analysis is a small enough fraction of the total design and building cost of large ships to be well worth it. Further, such vessels burn so much fuel that even a very small proportional reduction will easily repay the many thousands of dollars required for the analysis.

For small commercial vessels and yachts, however, such costly methods are seldom justified. The solution is to use a set of empirical formulas for predicting speed that have been refined over the years. These formulas take into account such fundamental factors as hull type and shape, displacement (total weight), and horsepower and, when used with common sense, can yield remarkably accurate speed estimates.

DETERMINING ACCURATE DISPLACEMENT OR WEIGHT FIGURES

One of the real keys to getting good results using these empirical methods is to use an honest and accurate figure for displacement* or weight. The most important factor governing speed is the power-to-weight ratio. The greater the power in proportion to weight, the greater the speed. It does no good to make accurate power estimates from engine performance curves, only to use optimistic figures or guesstimates for displacement.

---

*The displacement of a boat is its fully loaded weight. This is also equal to the weight of the volume of water the hull displaces or moves aside when it is lowered into the water or launched. Thus, it is only necessary to determine the volume of the hull to its load waterline and multiply that volume by the weight of seawater per cubic foot (64 lbs.) or per cubic centimeter (.0022 lb.) to find the true weight of the vessel.

For yachts, in particular, the current trend is to grossly underestimate weight in advertising and sales literature, frequently giving bare hull weight or light loaded displacement without fuel, crew, or stores. Such weights will yield unrealistically high speed predictions and result in choosing a propeller with too much pitch.

Weighing or Measuring to Find Displacement

The best way to determine the hull weight of a small trailerable boat is to drive the boat to a truck scale and weigh her. For larger craft the ideal solution is to contact the original designer and have him or her give you the displacement from the lines drawing based on the current, real flotation of the vessel. Measure the height from the sheer to the actual waterline at bow and stern, and the architect can tell how many inches down (or occasionally up) the boat is floating, and give you true displacement.

If you are considering a large vessel but have no information on her true displacement and lines, you have no choice but to measure her hull next time she is hauled out. It is not actually necessary to take off the craft's lines in detail, but simply to measure her at three sections. This simple procedure may be accomplished in a single afternoon, and is described in detail in Appendix A.

Remember that the displacement or weight you use in your speed calculation must be the actual, loaded weight of your vessel, as she will be in usual service. You must be sure to include the weights of:

1. Full crew and passengers.
2. All normal ship's stores and gear.
3. Two-thirds of all fuel and water tanks.
4. Two-thirds of all cargo.

Two-thirds of fuel, water, and cargo are used because this condition is a good, workable average of in-service loading. Most craft spend the majority of their operating hours with tanks and cargo at somewhere between 25 and 75 percent of capacity.

DETERMINING POWER REQUIRED FOR A GIVEN SPEED

Displacement Boats

Chart 2-1 gives boat speed (as speed-length ratio) as a function of power (in pounds per horsepower) for displacement and semidisplacement vessels. The curve is based on the formula:

Formula 2-1   *Displacement Speed Formula*

$$\text{SL RATIO} = 10.665 \div \sqrt[3]{\text{LB/SHP}}$$

Where

SL RATIO = Speed-length ratio and

SL RATIO = Kts $\div \sqrt{\text{WL}}$

Kts = Speed in knots = Boat speed or V

SHP = Shaft horsepower at propeller

LB = Displacement in pounds

WL = Waterline length in feet

Formula 2-1

The speed predicted by this formula assumes that the propeller gives between 50 and 60 percent efficiency, with 55 percent being a good average (see the section on Propeller Efficiency and Performance in Chapter 6).

CHART 2-1   DISPLACEMENT SPEED—INCLUDING SEMIDISPLACEMENT

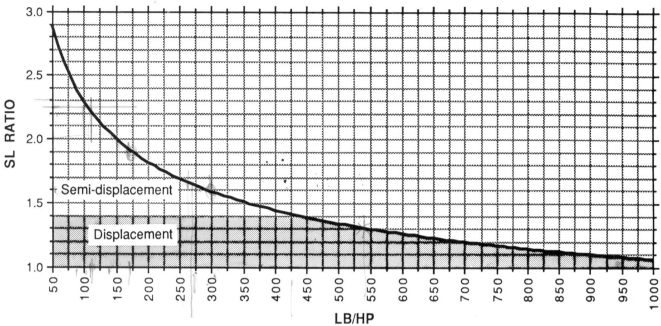

Chart 2-1. *This chart, an expansion of Formula 2-1, shows the power necessary to achieve a boat's known maximum speed-length ratio. It would be tempting to conclude from the chart that even a heavy-displacement hull can achieve SL ratios of 1.5 or higher given enough power, but in practice such an attempt would be unfeasible. For most moderate- to heavy-displacement vessels, incorporating more than one horsepower per 500 pounds or so of displacement in an effort to achieve SL ratios higher than 1.3 to 1.4 is neither practical nor economical. Heavy hulls designed with planing or semiplaning underbodies may be driven to semidisplacement speeds, but only at a great cost in fuel consumption and power (as detailed in the text that follows). For lightweight vessels, the commonsense approach is to determine the maximum SL ratio from Chart 2-2, and then determine the power necessary to achieve that speed from this chart.*

If for example you wished to determine the power required to drive the *Salty Bell,* a vessel of 220,000 pounds (99,790 kg) displacement and 70 feet (21.45 m) on the waterline at 11 knots, you would proceed as follows: Eleven knots on a 70-foot waterline gives a SL ratio of 1.31. [$(70 \text{ ft.})^{0.5} = 8.37 \text{ kts.}$, and 11 kts. ÷ 8.37 kts. = 1.31.] From Chart 2-1 or Formula 2-1, the pounds per horsepower (LB/HP) required is 533. Then, **220,000 lb. ÷ 533 LB/HP = 413 HP (308 kw)** at the propeller.

It is now important to remember the engine performance curves from Chapter 1. Although 413 HP (308 kw) is all that is required to produce 11 knots, this craft should operate continuously and economically at this speed. A vessel the size of *Salty Bell* will have an intermittent-duty marine diesel, which should be run at about 80 to 90 percent of top RPM, say 85 percent. Accordingly, we will need to specify a 485 HP (362 kw) engine for *Salty Bell* [**413 HP ÷ 0.85 = 485 HP (362 kw)**].

In addition to this, we have to remember that *Salty Bell* requires 413 HP (308 kw) at the propeller to operate at 11 knots. Accordingly, the horsepower required to run all auxiliary machinery driven off the main engine, as well as any power losses due to additional gearing (such as vee drives) or shaft bearings, should be added to the total engine horsepower.

In the case of *Salty Bell,* a further advantage of specifying an engine that operates continuously at 85 percent of top RPM is that such a power plant will provide that extra knot or so required for special circumstances. Few engines generate their top rated horsepower in actual service, but it would be reasonable to expect *Salty Bell*'s engine, rated at 485 HP (362 kw), to deliver bursts of 460 HP (343 kw) on demand. Chart 2-1 shows that this would give a top speed of about 11.7 knots.

Although Chart 2-1 goes up to SL ratios of 2.9, no ordinary nonplaning or displacement hull can achieve such speeds. The old rule-of-thumb that displacement hulls can go no faster than *hull speed* (1.34 times the square root of the waterline length in feet) should be kept in mind at all times. This rule has actually been found to be a bit conservative, and SL ratios 1.4 or 1.45 can be achieved in heavy vessels with fair lines, but at a great cost in power. The curve in Chart 2-1 rises very steeply after SL ratios of 1.5. For most ordinary displacement craft, there is no point in installing engines that give more than one horsepower at the propeller per 400 pounds of displacement (one kw per 240 kg). For operation at an SL ratio of 1.3 (normal or traditional hull speed), one horsepower per 550 pounds (one kw per 335 kg) at the propeller is sufficient. Tugs and trawlers that need to pull heavy loads require additional horsepower for towing. We will deal with them in detail in Chapter 8.

Semidisplacement Boats

Vessels that operate at SL ratios higher than 1.3 or 1.4 but below SL ratios of 2.5 to 3.0 (it is impossible to be precise here) are not true planing vessels. Such craft are called *semidisplacement* vessels or, occasionally, *semiplaning* vessels. You cannot convert a pure displacement-hulled craft into a semiplaning vessel simply by installing a larger engine. Such an exercise would be a waste of time and money. To reach semidisplacement speeds a boat must have a hull specifically designed for the purpose.

There are three significant factors that govern a hull's ability to reach semidisplacement speeds. One is the shape of her run (the shape of her underbody aft); the second is her displacement-length ratio, since vessels with very light displacements for their length can achieve higher speeds; and the third is a conglomeration of her seakeeping ability, strength, and comfort.

True planing hulls require flat underbodies aft, providing maximum area for useful planing surface. Semidisplacement hulls require some of this same characteristic, more if they are going very fast and less if their SL ratio is just a bit over hull speed. It is this feature that determines how fast a hull can be driven, and whether there is any point in installing engines that give more than one horsepower at the propeller per 400 pounds (one kw per 240 kg).

Buttock Angle Governs Speed Potential The best indicator of a hull's maximum speed potential is the angle her quarter-beam buttock makes with the waterline when she is at rest at her normal loading. Figure 2-1 shows the location of the quarter-beam buttock and how its angle should be measured. (Appendix A shows how to measure this directly from the hull, if no lines drawing is available.) These angles indicate speed potential for semidisplacement hulls as follows:

TABLE 2-1

Table 2-1   Buttock Angle vs SL Ratio Table

Buttock Angle	SL Ratio
less than 2°	2.5 or higher
4°	around 2
7°	around 1.5

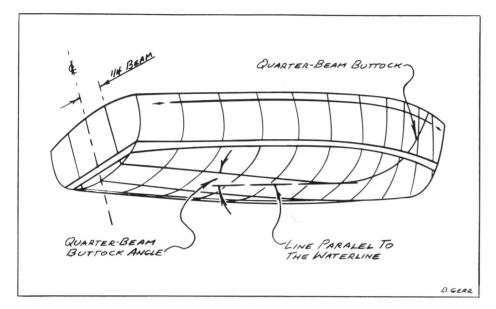

Figure 2-1

Quarter-beam buttock angle.

Hulls with quarter-beam buttock angles greater than 7 or 8 degrees can seldom if ever be made to go faster than an SL ratio of 1.4. If the buttock angles are less, then powering for the semidisplacement speed ranges shown above is worthwhile.

For example, if the same *Salty Bell* had a quarter-beam buttock angle of 3.8 degrees, we can interpolate from the table that she could be driven up to an SL ratio of about 2.1. This gives a speed, V, of 17.5 knots [**(70 ft.)$^{0.5}$ = 8.37 kts.,** and **2.1 SL ratio × 8.37 kts. = 17.57 kts**]. We can see from Chart 2-1 or Formula 2-1 that she would require one horsepower per 130 pounds to make this speed (one kw per 79 kg), which calls for 1,692 HP (1,262 kw) at the propeller [**220,000 lb. ÷ 130 LB/HP = 1,692 HP**]. It is immediately apparent that achieving high SL ratio speeds is very costly in power. While *Salty Bell*'s hull design makes the SL ratio of 2.1 achievable in theory, her 220,000 pounds' displacement makes this costly in practice.

Displacement-Length Ratio Affects Speed Potential Another indicator of a hull's speed potential is how light it is for its length on the waterline. Lightness is measured by the displacement-length or DL ratio, which is defined as follows:

Formula 2-2   Displacement-Length Ratio Formula

DL ratio = $DispT/(0.01 \times WL)^3$

Where:

DispT = Displacement in long tons of 2,240 pounds (a metric ton, mt, equals 1.016 long tons)

WL = Waterline length in feet

Formula 2-2

Chart 2-2 shows the maximum SL ratio a nonplaning hull can achieve with regard to its DL ratio. (A pure planing hull can achieve higher speeds than its DL ratio would indicate.) This curve is based on the following formula, derived by the author:

Formula 2-3   Maximum Speed-Length Ratio vs DL Ratio Formula

SL Ratio = 8.26 ÷ (DL RATIO)$^{0.311}$

Where:

SL RATIO = speed-length ratio

DL Ratio = displacement-length ratio

Formula 2-3

CHART 2-2   SL RATIO VS DL RATIO

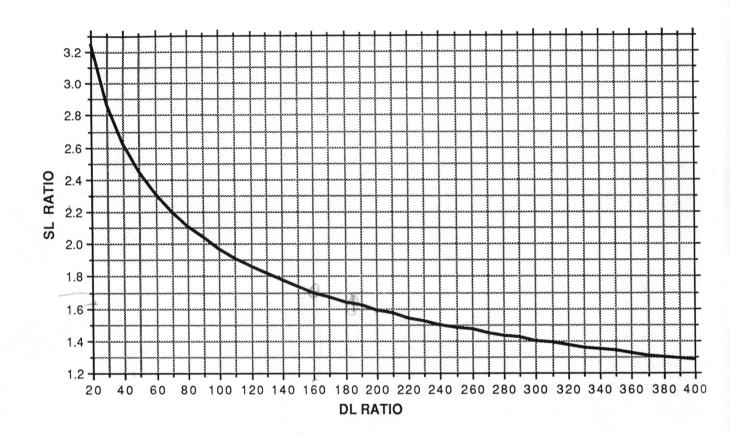

Chart 2-2.   *This chart, related to Formula 2-3, shows the maximum speed that a nonplaning hull can achieve as a function of its displacement-length ratio. Enter a hull's DL ratio, find the corresponding SL ratio, and then refer to Chart 2-1 for the power required to achieve this speed. There are three ways in which a vessel can achieve SL ratios significantly higher than about 1.45: One is by means of light weight; extremely light vessels having DL ratios of, say, 60 to 100 can achieve SL ratios upward of 2.0 even with comparatively steep buttock angles and other nonplaning hull characteristics. The second path to high SL ratios is a planing hull, which, given enough power, can achieve high speeds even with moderately heavy displacement. An example is* Salty Bell, *discussed in the accompanying text, which achieves an SL ratio of 2.1 despite a DL ratio of 286.* Salty Bell *essentially "breaks through" the displacement-hull limitations of the charted curve above by means of a good planing hull and a huge powerplant. She is typical of the crew vessels that carry men, provisions, and heavy equipment to offshore oil rigs. The third way to achieve high speeds is by far the most common—a combination of light weight and planing hull characteristics.*

Very low DL ratios permit high speeds (high SL ratios) without actually planing. In effect, the curve in Chart 2-2 indicates where the true hull speed occurs for vessels of differing DL ratios. Of course, the vast majority of nonplaning vessels—both pleasure and commercial—have DL ratios greater than 280. You can see from the chart that such vessels are limited to SL ratios below 1.42 or so. Such craft could make semidisplacement speeds only if their quarter-beam buttock angles were low and if they had tremendous power, as we discussed above.

If, however, we were considering a long, light vessel, *Sea Rocket,* 50 feet (15.2 m) on the waterline and only 30,000 pounds (13,608 kg) displacement, her DL ratio would be 107. From Chart 2-2 or Formula 2-2, we see that *Sea Rocket,* even with a comparatively steep quarter-beam buttock angle, could achieve SL ratios of about 1.9, or a V of 13.4 knots. We could then determine the horsepower required to drive her at this SL ratio from Chart 2-1.

Generally, flat or shallow buttock angles and light weight are conducive to high speed potential. A hull with these characteristics can be powered to operate at high speeds. Attempts to power vessels with buttock angles steeper than 8 degrees and displacement-length ratios over 290 to 300 to achieve SL ratios higher than 1.4 will not work.

Hull Strength and Seakindliness Affect Speed Potential   A final consideration in determining speed potential is the strength and seakindliness of the hull. Just as the power needed to drive a vessel increases geometrically with speed, so do the slamming and pounding loads. A shallow flat-bottom skiff will have a fairly low DL ratio and a very small buttock angle. Accordingly, such a vessel can easily be powered to reach semiplaning or planing speeds. Unfortunately, the pounding that such a craft will take outside smooth sheltered waters will be unacceptable to the crew and may even damage the hull. Before considering powering or repowering for high speeds, take into account the conditions the boat will operate in. Wide, flat-bottom hulls can be made to go very fast in smooth water, but if you operate in rough or choppy water regularly, you will be forced to slow down so often that the extra speed and power can seldom be used.

Planing Boats

Vessels that operate at speed-length ratios over 2.9 or 3 are true planing vessels. Such craft must have quarter-beam buttock angles under 2 degrees. Most modern planing vessels have quarter-beam buttock angles of 0 degrees. In other words, their quarter-beam buttock runs exactly parallel to the waterline. Light weight is critical as well. In theory, even very heavy craft could get up on a plane if they had enough power. The sheer size of the engines and the weight of fuel required to run them, however, makes light weight a practical necessity in all but very exceptional cases.

Chart 2-3 shows speed or V in knots attainable by power craft plotted against their power-to-weight ratio, LB/HP. These curves are based on Crouch's formula with the constant, C, adjusted to give speed in knots:

Formula 2-4   Crouch's Planing Speed Formula

Kts = C ÷ (LB/SHP)$^{0.5}$
Where:
Kts = Speed in knots = Boat speed, V
C = Constant chosen for the type of vessel being considered
LB = Displacement in pounds
SHP = Horsepower at the propeller shaft
The speed predicted by this formula assumes a propeller has been selected that gives between 50 and 60 percent efficiency, with 55 percent a good average (see Chapter 6).

Formula 2-4

CHART 2-3   PLANING SPEED

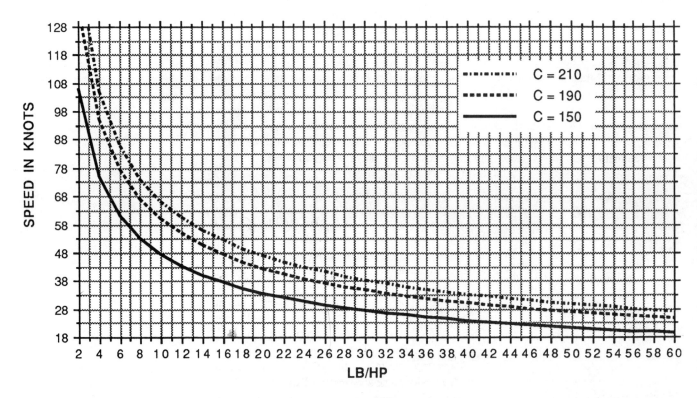

Chart 2-3.   *This chart, based on Formula 2-4, shows the speed attainable by planing craft as a function of available shaft horsepower. See Table 2-2 to estimate the appropriate C value with which to enter the table. This chart applies only to true planing vessels with quarter-beam buttock angles under 2 degrees and attainable speed-length ratios of at least 2.9 or 3.0.*

The key to getting reliable results from Crouch's formula is to use the correct constant, C. They should be chosen as follows:

TABLE 2-2   PLANING SPEED CHART CONSTANTS

TABLE 2-2

C	Type of Boat
150	average runabouts, cruisers, passenger vessels
190	high-speed runabouts, very light high-speed cruisers
210	race boat types
220	three-point hydroplanes, stepped hydroplanes
230	racing power catamarans and sea sleds

The vast majority of ordinary planing craft have C values of 150 or just slightly higher. Achieving the speeds given by C values of 190 or 200 requires a relatively narrow and efficient hull with very little tophamper, in the way of cabin structure. C values of 210 and above can only be applied to vessels that take this strategy to the ultimate degree. Additionally, such vessels require the benefit of small and well-formed propeller shafts and struts to reduce appendage drag to a minimum.

It is interesting to note that length is not considered at all in Crouch's formula. This may seem odd, but in practice, at planing speeds, power-to-weight ratio alone and not length is the overriding factor. Length cannot be neglected in your considerations, however. Longer, narrower boats (vessels with low DL ratios) should get higher C values, as we discussed above. Additionally, long, narrow boats with fine entries can be driven at high speeds in rough water, whereas wide, shallow-bodied craft cannot.

We can work through the example of the *Flying Spray,* a 35-foot (10.66 m) twin outboard runabout with weekender cabin forward. She is 30 feet (9.14 m) on the waterline, displaces 10,890 pounds (4,940 kg), and should operate at a V of 25 knots (28.8 MPH). Her displacement-length ratio of 180 is average to a bit light for a planing powerboat of this type. On the other hand, the lower unit housings of her outboards are not very efficient and create turbulence at the propellers, as well as appendage drag. Accordingly, an average C value of 150 is about right (from Table 2-2). From Chart 2-3 or Formula 2-4, we see that *Flying Spray* would require one horsepower per 36 pounds at the propeller. This gives 300 HP (224 kw) [**10,890 lb. ÷ 31 LB/HP = 302 HP**]. Since we want to operate continuously at this speed we have to figure on running at 70 percent of full throttle—outboards are light, high-speed engines. Thus, we need engines rated at a total of 430 HP (320 kw) [**300 HP ÷ 0.7 = 431 HP**]. Twin 215 to 220 HP (160 to 165 kw) outboards should do nicely.

At this point, we can start to answer another of the frequent questions we mentioned at the beginning of Chapter 1: "Why doesn't my boat reach the top speed claimed by the manufacturer?" You can run through the speed prediction methods outlined here to see how fast your boat should actually be capable of going with her real horsepower and at her real weight. Do not be surprised if you discover that, after taking your vessel's true weight into consideration (as opposed to the sales literature weight), her maximum cruising speed works out to less than claimed on the showroom floor. If, however, you discover that your engine has enough power to drive your vessel faster than you have been able to get her to go, then and only then is it time to consider a new propeller. This is particularly so if your engine cannot reach top RPMs, or if it reaches maximum RPMs well below full throttle. We will take a detailed look at propeller selection in Chapters 5 and 6.

Chapter 3
Propeller Anatomy
Parts and Definitions

Before we can begin to examine the propeller selection process in detail, we have to define clearly the propellers we will be choosing: How are they shaped? What are the differences and similarities between them? What types of propellers do we have to choose from, and which types are best suited for which service? We will answer these questions in the next two chapters.

PARTS OF THE PROPELLER

Hub The *hub* or *boss* of a propeller is the solid center disc, bored for the propeller shaft, to which the propeller blades are attached. Since the hub generates no drive, the ideal would be to eliminate it. As a practical matter, though, the hub can seldom be much less than 14 percent of the diameter in order for it to have sufficient strength.

Keyway Most propeller shafts transmit the torque from shaft to propeller through a *key*. The *key* is a long, slender rectangle of metal along the shaft that fits into a slot or *keyway* milled (cut away) into the interior at the hub. Standard keyway, shaft and hub dimensions may be found in Appendix C.

Blades The *propeller blades* are the twisted fins or foils that project out from the hub. It is the action of the blades that drives a boat through the water.

Blade Face and Blade Back The *blade face* is the high-pressure side, or *pressure face*, of the blade. It is the side facing aft, the side that pushes the water when the boat is moving forward. The *blade back* is the low pressure side or *suction face* of the blade, the side facing ahead.

Blade Root and Blade Tip The *blade root* is the point at which the blade attaches to the hub. The *blade tip* is the extreme outermost edge of the blade, as far from the propeller shaft center as possible.

Leading and Trailing Edges The *leading edge* of a blade is the edge of the blade that cleaves the water. The *trailing edge* is the edge from which the water streams away.

ROTATION OR HAND

A critical aspect of propeller shape is its *hand*. A propeller that drives a boat forward when it rotates clockwise, as viewed from astern, is called a *right-handed propeller*. By the same token, a propeller that rotates counterclockwise, as viewed from astern, is *left-handed*. You can tell a right-handed propeller from a left-handed propeller just by looking at it. As you view the propeller from astern, the leading edges of the blades will always be farther away from you than the trailing edges. If the leading edges are to your right,

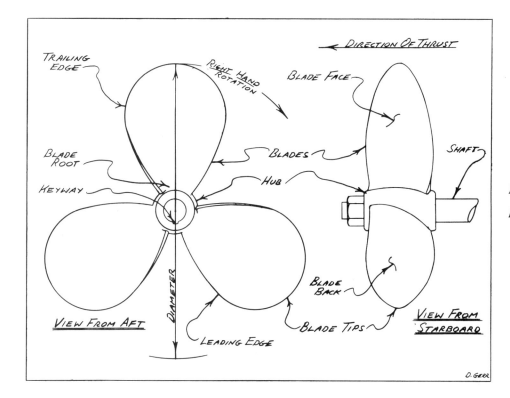

Figure 3-1

Propeller anatomy.

the propeller rotates clockwise and is a right-handed propeller. If the converse is true, it is a left-handed propeller.

Propeller hand can never be changed. If you obtain a propeller of the wrong hand for your installation, you simply have to replace it with one that has the correct hand. You cannot change the hand by turning the propeller backwards.

Right-handed propellers are almost, but not quite, universal on single-screw vessels. In twin-screw installations, propellers and engines of opposite hand are used port and starboard. A single right-handed propeller will tend to push the stern of a vessel to star-

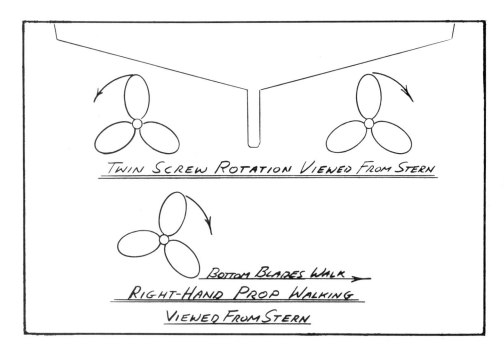

Figure 3-2

Propellers "walk" in the direction of rotation.

board when going forward (to port going astern). The reason—in simple terms—is that the water at the bottom of the propeller is a bit denser and freer to flow (there's no hull above it) than at the top of the propeller. This makes the lower blades a bit more effective, so the propeller and the stern "walk" sideways in the direction of rotation.

On a twin-screw craft the propellers should be out-turning. The starboard or right propeller should be right-handed, and the port or left propeller should be left-handed. This gives the best handling and, if you operate on one engine, the walking effect of each propeller helps counteract the fact that the shaft is off center. Twin-screw vessels with propellers of the same hand can experience serious handling problems.

THE THREE BASIC CHARACTERISTICS

Diameter, revolutions per minute and *pitch* are the three most significant factors affecting propeller performance and efficiency. Although many other variables need to be considered, the vast majority of calculations for selecting a suitable propeller revolve around these three characteristics.

Diameter

The most obvious characteristic of any propeller is its *diameter (D)*. This is simply the distance across the circle swept by the extreme tips of the propeller blades.

Effects of Diameter Diameter is the single most critical factor in determining the amount of power that a propeller absorbs and transmits. It is thus the most important single factor in determining the amount of thrust delivered.

For the vast majority of installations, the larger the diameter the greater the efficiency. The only exception is for high-speed vessels—over 35 knots or so—in which the extra wetted surface of large-diameter shafts, bearings, and so on causes excessive drag. A small increase in diameter dramatically increases thrust and *torque* load (see section on torque in Chapter 1) on the engine and shaft. For this reason, the larger the diameter, the slower the shaft RPM must be. In theory, a propeller with a diameter as large as one-third of the beam of the vessel and turning at only a dozen or so RPMs is most efficient. Practical limits on draft, hull shape, RPMs and reduction gear losses restrict diameter to far less than this.

Revolutions per Minute

Revolutions per minute (RPM or N) is the number of full turns or rotations that a propeller makes in a single minute. Since the propeller rotates at the same speed as the propeller shaft, this is often called *shaft RPM* or *tail-shaft RPM*.

Shaft RPM is frequently very different from engine RPM, the speed at which the engine crankshaft turns at a given throttle setting. On the vast majority of installations, a *reduction gear* is fitted between the crankshaft and the tail or propeller shaft. The purpose of the reduction gear is to reduce RPMs at the propeller so that a larger-diameter, more efficient propeller may be used with an economical, compact, high-speed engine.

Some common reduction ratios are 2:1, 2.4:1 and 3:1; however, a vast number of reduction gears are available with a wide selection of ratios. In practice, it is frequently most economical to match the propeller to the standard reduction gears supplied by the engine manufacturer for their various engine models. When this is not possible, you can find a number of companies that specialize in producing marine reduction and reverse gear for a variety of special installations. In many cases, the gears may also serve to solve engine placement problems. Vee drives, offset drives and angled drives can combine a reduction gear with radical changes in shaft direction.

Shaft speed or RPM may be calculated simply by dividing the engine or crankshaft RPM by the reduction ratio. For example, an engine operating at 3,000 RPMs with a 2.4:1 reduction gear would have a shaft RPM of 1,250 [**3,000 RPMs ÷ 2.4 reduction = 1,250 RPMs**].

The reduction gear mechanism does absorb or waste power—roughly 3 percent—so for the ultimate in efficiency, the ideal would be to eliminate the reduction gear altogether. This is seldom done because engines able to develop sufficient power at low enough speeds are excessively large and heavy, using up valuable interior hull space.

High-speed craft, however, often use propellers that operate at engine speed. In fact, in some very high-speed racing vessels, it is necessary to increase tail-shaft RPMs above those of the crankshaft. Such vessels are fitted with *step-up gears*.

Effects of RPM   Generally, high RPMs are not conducive to efficiency except on very high-speed craft. For vessels operating under 35 knots, lowering the RPMs permits a larger-diameter propeller to be swung with the same size and weight of engine and the same fuel consumption. Since a larger-diameter propeller is more efficient in producing thrust, lower RPMs are generally desirable for most installations.

On high-speed vessels, where it is important to keep the size of the propeller and its supporting structure small to reduce appendage drag, higher RPMs and thus smaller propellers, propeller shafts and struts can be beneficial.

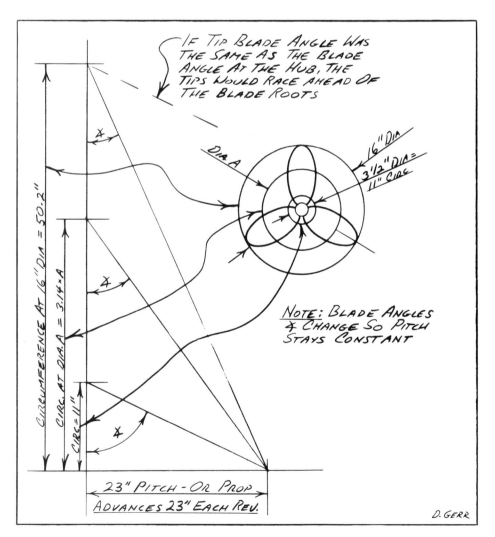

Figure 3-3

Blade twist and propeller pitch.

Pitch

The term *pitch (P)* comes from the old screw analogy used to approximate propeller action. This analogy says that a propeller screws itself through the water much as a wood screw works itself into soft pine. In fact, the proper term for a propeller is *screw propeller.*

Face Pitch Just as a wood screw does, the propeller will—in theory—drive forward a certain fixed distance for each complete revolution. (See also the discussion of *virtual pitch* below.) This distance is called *pitch.* A more precise term for this is *face pitch,* as this defines the angles of the blade faces. If the propeller moves forward 10 inches (254 mm) for every complete turn, it has a 10-inch pitch. Since the propeller is firmly attached to its propeller shaft, it pushes the shaft forward by the same distance. In turn, the shaft pushes on a thrust bearing that imparts force against the hull itself. On the majority of small- to medium-sized engines, the thrust bearing is in the gearbox, or transmission, attached to the engine.

In each revolution, though, the propeller actually pushes the boat forward less distance than its *nominal* face pitch. The difference between the nominal pitch and the *actual* distance traveled is called *slip.* (We'll examine this in detail in Chapters 5 and 6.)

As with any other rotating object, the inner part of the propeller (near the hub) travels much less distance during each full turn than the tips. For, say, a propeller with 16-inch (406.4 mm) diameter, the tips would be traveling along a 50.26-inch (1276.6 mm) circumference. By contrast, the root of the blades, right by the hub, would only be traveling along an 11-inch (279.4 mm) circumference each revolution. This is a very substantial difference. Since the tips of the blades cannot be allowed to race ahead of the inner part

Figure 3-4

A standard three-bladed propeller, showing the characteristic blade twist that gives constant, or helical, pitch.

(Courtesy of W.H. Den Ouden Vetus)

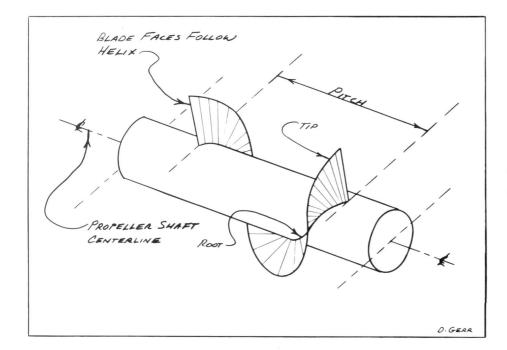

BLADE FACES FOLLOW HELIX

PITCH

TIP

PROPELLER SHAFT CENTERLINE

ROOT

a

O. GERR

Figure 3-5

Constant pitch blade helix.

of the propeller, they are given a shallower angle. In this way, the tips end up at the same place as the blade roots every full turn. Carrying this principle evenly all the way along the length of the blades gives them their characteristic twist.

It's good to remember that the *pitch* of a propeller is not the same as its *blade angles*. Figure 3-6A is a sectional view of a propeller blade at some distance out from the shaft centerline, say 70 percent of the distance to the blade tip. The blade is turning up out of the plane of the page above the shaft centerline and down into the page below the shaft centerline. The blade angle for this section is angle *a*, the angle between the blade face and a plane perpendicular to the shaft centerline. This angle will vary all along the blade, as shown in Figure 3-6B, to keep pitch constant. In fact, the accurate name of the pitch we have been describing is *constant face pitch*—"constant" because the pitch (unlike the blade angles) does not change, and "face" because it really applies to the face of the blade alone. The faces of the blades of a propeller with constant face pitch describe a perfect or true helix with a pitch equal to the nominal pitch of the propeller.

Variable-Pitch Propellers   The majority of propellers have blades with essentially constant pitch, but a few specialized propellers have blades with pitch that changes substantially from root to tip. This means that the blade angles do not vary in such a way as to keep pitch constant. The principal reason for these *variable-pitch propellers* is to take advantage of varying speeds of water flow to the propeller—as measured radially out from the hub—due to the interference of the hull ahead.

Propellers with truly variable pitch are outside the scope of this book. This type of installation is called for only on large vessels with special need for the ultimate in efficiency. However, many modern propellers do have a small amount of variable pitch introduced near the blade root as a result of changing blade section. Frequently, they also reduce the pitch near the tip of the blades slightly from that of a theoretical helix. This is called *pitch relief* or *tip unloading,* and it has been found to reduce the tendency for *cavitation* to start at the propeller tips (see Chapter 4).

Controllable–Pitch Propellers   The term *controllable-pitch propeller* sounds similar to variable-pitch propeller, but actually it refers to a completely different concept. A con-

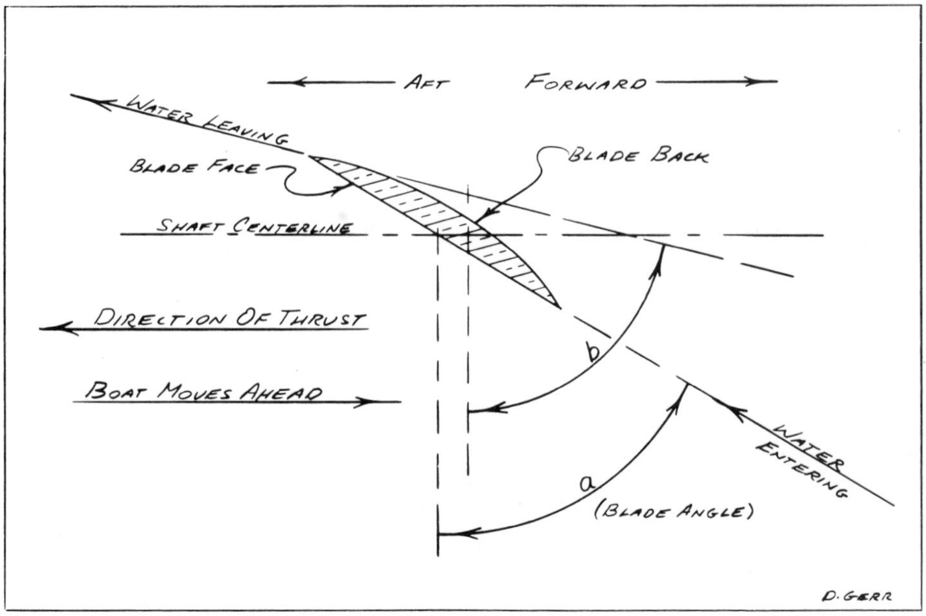

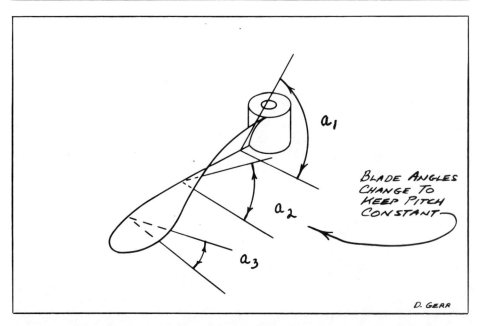

Figure 3-6A

Virtual pitch angle.

Figure 3-6B

The blade angle a changes continuously from root to tip in order to keep the pitch constant.

trollable-pitch propeller allows the operator to change the pitch of the propeller blades at will while underway. Usually, a hydraulic mechanism or a direct mechanical linkage permits rotation of the blades around the individual blade axes, independent of shaft revolutions.

Controllable-pitch propellers offer significant advantages in economy of operation for vessels that operate under varying conditions of load, such as tugs, trawlers and motorsailers. This is because the operator can adjust pitch to suit the thrust required for, say, running free or towing. Obviously, however, controllable-pitch propellers are considerably more expensive and complicated than ordinary solid propellers. We will deal with them at greater length in Chapter 8.

Virtual Pitch The final consideration in pitch is called *virtual* or *hydrodynamic pitch*. In reality, a propeller does not operate like a wood screw, although the analogy is useful. Water enters the propeller blades at an angle (angle *a* in Figure 3-6) relative to a plane at right angles to the shaft line, and leaves the trailing edge of the blades at a differing angle, *b*. This angle varies all along the length of the blades, and the average of these differing angles is the virtual pitch. The virtual pitch is the real or true pitch of a propeller. It is never specified by manufacturers; its importance lies in the fact (see below) that it may vary among propellers having the same face pitch, and the behavior of these propellers in use will vary somewhat as a consequence.

Analysis Pitch, P_0 Like virtual pitch, *analysis pitch, (P_0),* also called *experimental pitch,* is another way of measuring true or effective pitch. *Analysis pitch* is the pitch of a propeller as measured by the water speed and RPM at which the propeller cannot keep up with the water flow—in other words, the speed and RPM when thrust falls to zero.

When at a given speed through the wake, *Va* (see Chapter 6), at a given RPM, the propeller thrust vanishes, the analysis pitch, P_0 (in feet) is 101.33 times the speed through the wake (in knots) divided by the RPMs at zero thrust, N_0. For a propeller delivering zero thrust at 2,800 RPM through a 21-knot wake, the analysis pitch would be 0.76 feet or 9 inches (231.5 mm) [**101.33 × 21 knots ÷ 2800 RPMs = 0.76 ft = 9 in**].

Formula 3-1   Analysis Pitch Formula

Analysis pitch = P_0 (in feet)

$P_0 = 101.33 Va \div N_0$

Where:

Va = speed in knots through wake at zero thrust

N_0 = shaft RPM at zero thrust

Formula 3-1

Pitch Comparisons Increasing blade thickness and increasing blade width both have the effect of increasing the virtual pitch. Since propeller manufacturers specify their propellers based on face pitch—it would be a prohibitively complex undertaking to calculate virtual pitch—it is important to compare propellers of comparable blade thickness, blade pattern, and width; otherwise their real or virtual pitches will be different even though their specified face pitches are the same.

Even measuring simple face pitch poses some problems. Since the blade angles vary all along the length of the blades, from the root to the tip, you would get a different pitch measurement depending on where you took the measurement. By convention, however, the face pitch is always measured at 70 percent of the radius out from the shaft center. For instance, a 44-inch (1117.6 mm) diameter propeller would have its face pitch measured 15.4 inches (391.16 mm) out from the shaft center [**44″ diameter ÷ 2 = 22″ radius, and 22″ × 0.7 = 15.4″**].

Pitch Ratio Pitch is defined in terms of inches or millimeters; however, it is also very useful to define pitch as a ratio of diameter—*pitch-diameter ratio, pitch ratio* or *p/d ratio*. A 20-inch (508 mm) diameter propeller with a pitch of 18 inches (457.2 mm) has a pitch ratio of 0.9 [**18″ ÷ 20″ = 0.9**].

Formula 3-2   Pitch Ratio Formula

Pitch ratio = P/D

Where:

P = pitch

D = diameter

Formula 3-2

Pitch ratios generally fall between 0.5 and 2.5; however, the vast majority of vessels operate best with propellers having pitch ratios between 0.8 and 1.8. Very roughly, a pitch ratio of 0.8 can be expected to produce efficiencies of around 0.65, while pitch ratios of around 1.4 can result in efficiencies as high as 0.74. At pitch ratios higher than 1.5, efficiency generally starts to fall off. Lower pitch ratios are usually suited to lower-speed craft, and higher pitch ratios are best for high-speed craft.

A propeller that has a pitch ratio of 1.0—say, an 18-inch (457.2 mm) diameter and 18-inch (457.2 mm) pitch—is said to be a *square wheel*. In the past, some designers have given this proportion a sort of mystic importance. In practice, though, there is nothing special about a square wheel, although a pitch ratio of 1.0 is in a reasonably efficient operating regime.

Effects of Pitch   Pitch converts the torque of the propeller shaft to thrust by deflecting or accelerating water astern. The formula describing this is Newton's Second Law: force (or thrust) equals mass times acceleration, or $F = MA$. In this light, a propeller drives a vessel forward exactly as a jet engine or rocket motor propels a plane or missile. The force or thrust is directly proportional to the mass or weight of water moved astern times the acceleration of that mass.

Since the mass being accelerated is water, thrust can be calculated as follows:

Formula 3-3   Theoretical Thrust Formula

Formula 3-3

Thrust = Force, F

$F = MA$ or

$F = W/g\,(V_0 - V_1)$

Where:

W = weight in pounds of the column of water accelerated astern by the propeller

g = the acceleration of gravity, 32.2 ft./sec.^{2}

V_0 = velocity of water before entering propeller in feet per second

V_1 = velocity of water after leaving propeller in feet per second

M = mass in slugs

A = acceleration in feet per second squared

In a similar fashion, the speed of the vessel is proportional to the momentum of the water according to the law of conservation of momentum, or $M_1 V_1 = M_2 V_2$. In other words, the mass of water accelerated astern times its velocity will equal the mass of the vessel accelerated forward times its velocity. This relationship is very much complicated by the resistance of the water surrounding the hull, which is constantly working to slow it.

Even on a large diameter propeller, wide round "blades" like baseball bats, without pitch or angle of attack, would not accelerate any water astern and so would do nothing but generate tremendous churning. Such a propeller would not drive a boat forward at all. Conversely, ordinary blades with too much pitch would attempt to force more water astern more quickly than the engine could accommodate. This would simply place such a load on the engine that it would slow and never reach its maximum RPM or rated output power. This is both inefficient and potentially damaging to the engine.

The fundamental task in selecting a propeller is to choose a pitch and diameter that will generate the maximum thrust possible at normal operating speeds without overloading the engine. Increasing pitch increases thrust, but increasing pitch too much reduces the efficiency of the engine and propeller combination by slowing the engine. On the other hand, while too little pitch will not overload or slow the engine, it will not accelerate as much water astern and thus will not generate maximum possible thrust or speed.

Chapter 4
Blade Characteristics

Blade Shape, Cavitation, Special Propellers, and Rules of Thumb

In the preceding chapter, we described the parts of a propeller, defined its overall dimensions, and saw how blades are twisted to create the pitch that generates thrust. Nevertheless, it's important to bear in mind that two propellers of identical diameter and pitch could be quite different. For instance, one propeller could have very wide blades, and the other narrow or skinny blades. It's intuitively obvious that the wider-bladed propeller would absorb more thrust and horsepower, but we need to be able to define blade area, shape and width exactly to specify the correct propeller for a specific application. (Blade area is particularly important in determining if a propeller will cavitate or not.)

Likewise, the blades themselves may have different sectional shapes—differing thicknesses and contours—or, of course, two propellers of the same diameter could have a differing number of blades. Again, we need to be able to understand and describe all these variables exactly in choosing a propeller. Furthermore, there are specialized propellers, such as controllable-pitch propellers and ducted propellers, that are particularly suited to specific applications.

CHARACTERISTICS OF BLADES

Number of Blades

Let's consider the question: How many blades? Surprisingly, the ideal is one. A single blade does not have other blades disturbing the water flow ahead of it. Unfortunately, trying to get a single-bladed propeller to balance is like trying to clap with one hand. Having two blades is the logical answer. Both sailboats trying to reduce drag and very high-speed powerboats frequently use two-bladed propellers. The problem with two-bladed propellers for most vessels is that such propellers require very large diameters to get the blade area required for effective thrust. As a result, three-bladed propellers have generally proven to be the best compromise between balance, blade area and efficiency.

Effects of Multiple Blades

Four- or five-bladed propellers—and propellers with even more blades—are useful for two reasons. First, their extra blades create more total blade area with the same or less diameter. Accordingly, an installation that needed a 20-inch (508 mm) three-bladed propeller but only had room for an 18-incher (457.2 mm) could obtain sufficient thrust from, say, a properly sized four-bladed propeller. The four-blader, however, would seldom be as efficient as the three-blader because the closer blades create additional turbulence, literally scrambling up each other's water flow.

Another reason to use more than three blades is to reduce vibration. If a propeller is in the habit of producing annoying, rhythmic thumping and humming, a propeller with more blades will often go a long way toward curing the problem. Every time the blades of the propeller pass under the hull or by the strut, they cause a change in pressure that causes a push (or a suction). If the push is strong enough it generates a bang. Lots of rapid bangs equals vibration.

The blades of a three-bladed propeller turning at 1,000 RPMs pass under the stern 3,000 times every minute, or 50 times a second—a vibration of 50 cycles per second (cps), or 50 Hz (hertz). Switching to a four-bladed propeller—still at 1,000 RPMs—would change this to 4,000 times a minute, or 66 cps. The more rapid the cycles, the smoother the feel—and the less likely the hull is to resonate (amplify the sound like the body of a guitar) with the vibration.

For reducing vibration, there is a further advantage to substituting a propeller with more blades and consequently smaller diameter. If, for example, a 30-inch (762 mm) diameter three-bladed propeller were replaced with a 28-inch (711 mm) four-bladed propeller, the tip clearance (the distance between the hull and the propeller blades) would increase by 1 inch (25 mm). If the original tip clearance had been 4.5 inches (114 mm), this would amount to a 22 percent increase. Increasing tip clearance will greatly reduce the force of the pushes that cause vibration. When dealing with an installation that has been producing severe vibration, such an approach can be very effective in solving the problem.

Blade Area—Projected and Developed (Ap and Ad)

Blade area is the surface area of the individual propeller blades. The blade area has a direct effect on a propeller's tendency to cavitate and on the power it absorbs, but because of the complex shape of propeller blades, it is not easy to measure directly. The most common two measurements are *projected blade area,* Ap, and *developed blade area,* Ad (also called *expanded blade area*). Projected blade area is the area of the blades as viewed from directly astern. Another way to visualize this is as the area of the silhouette or shadow cast by the blades with a light shining from directly ahead.

Since the blades are twisted, the projected blade area is always less than the true blade area (the expanded or developed area). To find the developed blade area, a designer systematically expands (straightens out) the curved and twisted area on a drawing and measures this expanded area. This is the same as carefully fitting a piece of paper flush against the surface of the blade, cutting it to match the blade outline, laying it out flat on

---

CHART 4-1   DEVELOPED AREA TO PROJECTED AREA CONVERSION

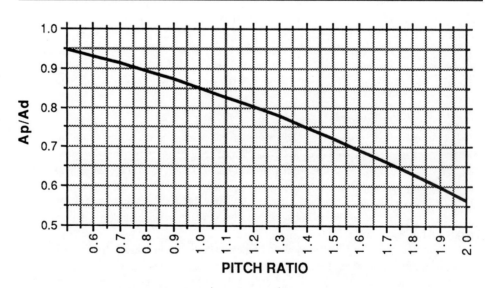

Chart 4-1. *This chart, based on Formula 4-1, plots the developed-area to projected-area ratio against the pitch ratio. If, for example, you know the projected area (Ap) and the pitch ratio, you can find the developed area (Ad) by dividing Ap by the factor shown in the chart.*

the table and measuring the area. (See Appendix B.) Developed blade area is the area most frequently used in making propeller calculations, since it represents the true total area actually absorbing thrust.

Developed Area to Projected Area Conversion Chart 4-1 gives the approximate ratio of the developed area to the projected area as plotted against the pitch ratio. If you know the developed area of a propeller with, say, a pitch ratio of 1.2, then Chart 4-1 gives the Ap/Ad ratio as 0.8. Accordingly, if the developed area (Ad) were 1,000 square inches (6452 cm²), the projected area (Ap) would be 800 square inches (5162 cm²). If the projected area is known, you can find the developed area by dividing by the Ap/Ad factor from Chart 4-1. For instance, if the Ap (projected area) of a propeller with a pitch ratio of 0.9 is 500 square inches (3227 cm²), then the Ad (developed area) would be 573 square inches (3696 cm²). (The factor from the chart is 0.87, and **500 sq. in. ÷ 0.87 = 573 sq. in.**)

Chart 4-1 is based on the following formula:

Formula 4-1   Developed Area to Projected Area Formula

Ap/Ad = 1.0125 − (0.1 × PR) − (0.0625 × PR²)
Where:
Ap/Ad = Approximate ratio of projected area to developed area
PR = Pitch ratio of propeller

Formula 4-1

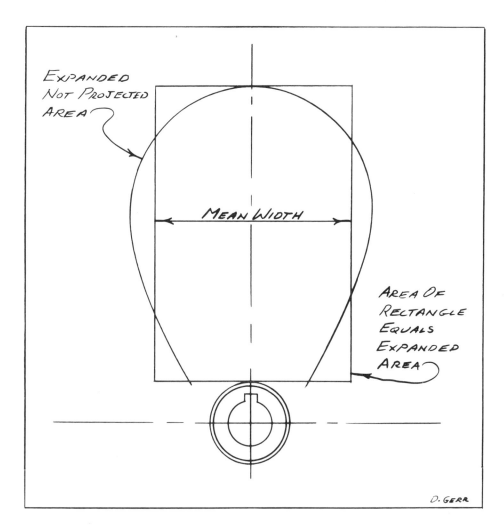

Figure 4-1

Determining the mean width of a propeller blade.

Mean-Width Ratio or MWR In order to compare propellers of different diameters, a number of ratios describing blade area are used. The *mean width* of a propeller blade is the width of a rectangle that has the same area as the blade and the same length of the blade from root to tip—*not from shaft centerline*. Thus, a propeller 74 inches (1879.6 mm) in diameter with an 11-inch (279.4 mm) diameter hub would have a blade height of 31.5 inches (800.1 mm) [**74 in.–11 in. = 63 in.**, and **63 in. ÷ 2 = 31.5 in.**]. If the expanded blade area is 656 square inches (4232 cm²), the mean width is 20.82 inches (528.83 mm) [**656 in.² ÷ 31.5 in. = 20.82 in.**]. The *mean-width ratio* or *MWR* is simply the mean width divided by the diameter, or in this case, **MWR = 0.28 (20.82 in. ÷ 74 in. = 0.28)**.

Formula 4-2 Mean-Width Ratio Formula

Formula 4-2

Mean-width ratio = MWR
MWR = average blade width ÷ D or
MWR = (expanded area of one blade ÷ blade height from root to tip) ÷ D
Where:
D = diameter

Mean-width ratios usually vary from about 0.2 to 0.55. MWRs of around 0.35 are considered normal for most moderate- to high-speed applications. Higher mean-width ratios are used for highly loaded propellers to reduce cavitation or to keep diameter down. Small mean-width ratios are most frequently used on propellers with more than three blades to keep the total blade area small.

Disc-Area Ratio or DAR Another useful measure of propeller blade area is the *disc area,* the area of the circle described by the maximum propeller diameter. For example, a 42-inch (1066.8 mm) diameter propeller would have a disc area of 1,385.43 square inches (8932 cm²) [**π42 in.² ÷ 4 = 1,385.43 in.²**].

The *disc-area ratio* is simply the total developed area of all the blades divided by the disc area. Thus, if the 42-inch (1066.8 mm) propeller above had an expanded area of 242 square inches (1561 cm²) per blade, and had three blades, its disc-area ratio would be 0.51 [**242 in.² × 3 blades = 726 in.²**, and **726 in.² ÷ 1,385.43 in.² = 0.51.**].

Formula 4-3 Disc-Area Formula

Formula 4-3

Disc area = πD² ÷ 4   (or 0.7854D²)
Disc-Area Ratio = DAR
DAR = expanded area of all blades ÷ disc area
Where:
D = diameter
π≈3.14

Figure 4-2

Disc area of a propeller.

DISC AREA IS AREA OF A CIRCLE WITH SAME DIA AS PROP

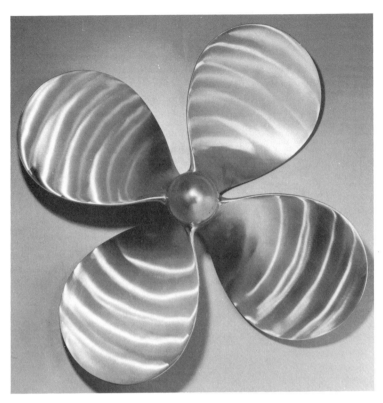

Figure 4-3

A four-bladed propeller with wide, non-skewed blades of fully ogival (flat-faced) section. The mean-width ratio of the blades is 0.33, and the disc-area ratio is 0.61. Such a propeller is best suited to low-speed, high-thrust applications—workboats, trawlers, tugs, and so on. The three-bladed pattern of this propeller has the same MWR but a DAR of 0.50. The smaller blade area of the three-blader makes it more suitable for lighter displacement motor cruisers and moderate speed commuters.

(Courtesy of The Michigan Wheel Company)

Effects of Blade Area A number of conflicting factors affect the choice of blade area. Propeller blades actually behave largely like airfoils or hydrofoils. (A foil is a shape specifically designed to generate thrust or lift when moving through a fluid.) Longer, narrower blades are theoretically more efficient. Unfortunately, very long, narrow blades call for large diameters and low RPMs, which are seldom practical.

Figure 4-4

A four-bladed propeller with narrow, non-skewed blades of fully ogival (flat-faced) section. The mean-width ratio of the blades is 0.21, and the disc-area ratio is 0.43. Propellers such as this are intended to replace three-bladed propellers of the same diameter but with wider blades (blades of the more normal mean-width ratio of between 0.30 and 0.35). This provides the additional smoothness of four blades without the loss of efficiency from decreased diameter, though there is still some loss of efficiency from the blades' being closer together. Such a propeller cannot be used if it does not provide sufficient blade area to prevent cavitation.

(Courtesy of The Michigan Wheel Company)

Since propeller thrust is actually created by water pressure on the blades, this pressure can be described in terms of pounds per square inch (kilograms per square centimeter). Blades with pressures that are too high tend to lose efficiency and to cavitate (see the discussion later in this chapter). Accordingly, lower blade pressures are desirable. Thus, to create a given thrust in the same diameter propeller, it's necessary to increase blade area. Wider blades, though, increase the turbulence between blades and have greater induced drag (tip vortexes). Years of experiment have shown that for most average applications, mean-width ratios should vary from about 0.2 to 0.5, and disc-area ratios from about 0.4 to 0.7. Generally, the smaller the diameter and the higher the RPM, the wider the blades; thus, the higher the MWR and DAR.

Relationships of MWR, DAR, and Developed Area

Knowing just the propeller diameter, the number of blades, and either the mean-width ratio or the disc-area ratio of the blades enables us to determine the total blade area exactly. We will use this information frequently in checking for cavitation. Mean-width ratio also defines disc-area ratio (and vise versa), as follows:

Formula 4-4   Disc-Area Ratio vs Mean-Width Ratio

DAR = No. of Blades × 0.51 × MWR

or

$$MWR = \frac{DAR}{No.\ of\ Blades \times 0.51}$$

Formula 4-4

Where:

DAR = Disc-area ratio

MWR = Mean-width ratio

Note: These ratios assume a hub that is 20 percent of overall diameter, which is very close to average. Small propellers for pleasure craft may have slightly smaller hubs, while heavy, workboat propellers, particularly controllable-pitch propellers, may have slightly larger hubs.

From this formula we find that, for instance, a three-bladed propeller with a MWR of 0.33 has a DAR of 0.5 [**3 blades × 0.51 × 0.33 MWR = 0.5 DAR**].

Total developed area may be found from the disc-area ratio as follows:

Formula 4-5   Developed Area vs Disc-Area Ratio Formula

Formula 4-5

Ad = π × (D/2)² × DAR

Total developed area may also be found from the mean-width ratio, as follows:

Formula 4-6   Developed Area vs Mean-Width Ratio Formula

Ad = π × (D/2)² × MWR × 0.51 × No. of Blades

Where, for both of the above formulas:

Formula 4-6

Ad = Developed area

D = Diameter

DAR = Disc-area ratio

MWR = Mean-width ratio

π≈3.14

Thus a four-bladed propeller with a MWR of 0.4 and a diameter of 42 inches (1,066 mm) would have a developed area of 1,025 square inches (6613 cm²) [**3.14 × (42 in./2)² × 0.4 MWR × 0.51 × 4 Blades = 1,024.8 in²**].

CHART 4-2   DEVELOPED AREA VS DIAMETER

A

Three-Bladed 12″–36″

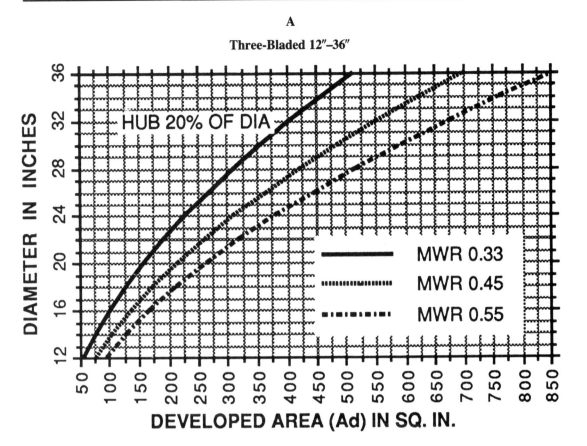

Three-Bladed 36″–72″

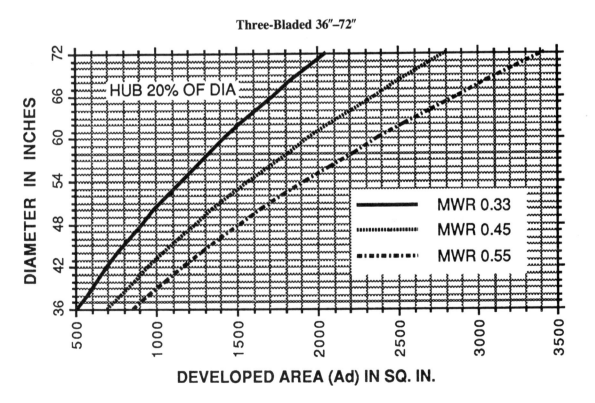

B

Three-Bladed 72″–96″

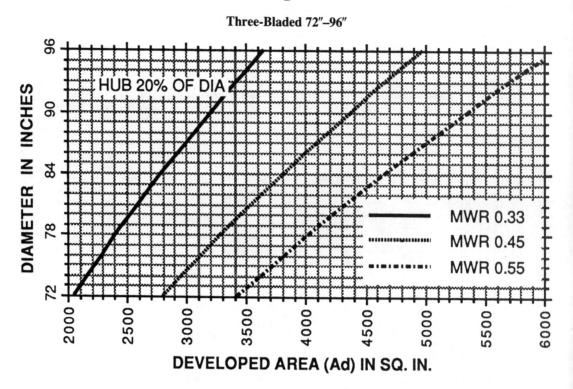

Four-Bladed 12″–36″

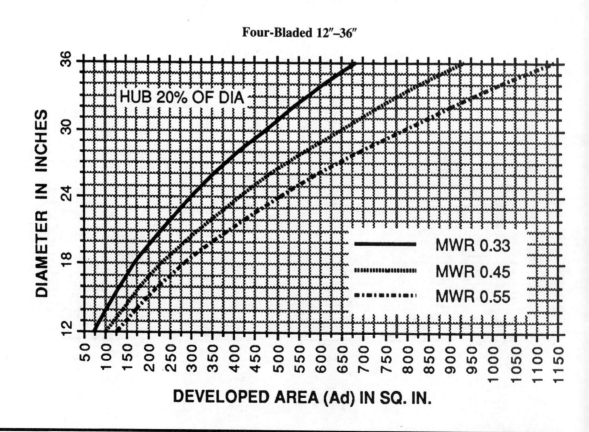

C

Four-Bladed 36″–72″

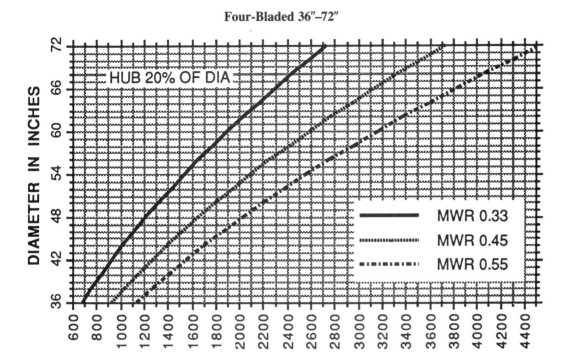

Four-Bladed 72″–96″

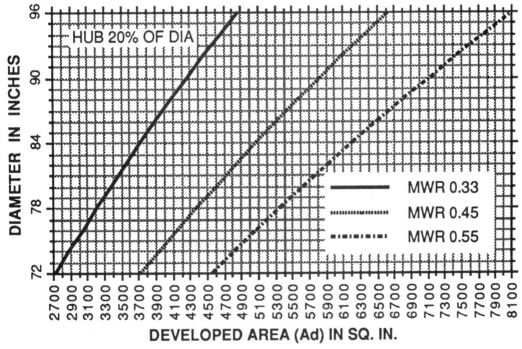

Chart 4-2A, B, and C. *These charts, based on Formula 4-5, give the developed or expanded area of the blades as a function of diameter, mean-width ratio, and number of blades. Developed area is useful to know when assessing the possibility of cavitation. The values in the charts are based on a propeller hub diameter 20 percent of the overall diameter, which is accurate for the vast majority of standard-pattern propellers. If an adjustment is necessary, use Formula 4-7.*

Charts 4-2a, b, and c plot developed or expanded area against diameter in inches for three- and four-bladed propellers of varying mean-width ratios based on Formula 4-5. Remember that these values are predicated on an average hub sized at 20 percent of overall diameter. To find area from MWR for propellers of *any* hub dimension, the following formula should be used:

Formula 4-7 Developed Area for Any Hub Diameter and MWR Formula

$$Ad = MWR \times D \times (1\text{-hub}\%) \times D/2 \times \text{No. of Blades, or}$$

$$Ad = MWR \times \frac{D^2}{2} \times (1\text{-hub}\%) \times \text{No. of Blades}$$

Formula 4-7

Where:

Ad = Developed area

MWR = Mean width ratio

D = Diameter

hub% = Maximum hub diameter divided by overall diameter, D

Blade Section Shape

If you cut or slice a blade at right angles to the radius—lopping off, say, the outer third—you are looking at a section through the propeller blade. Such sections have a carefully

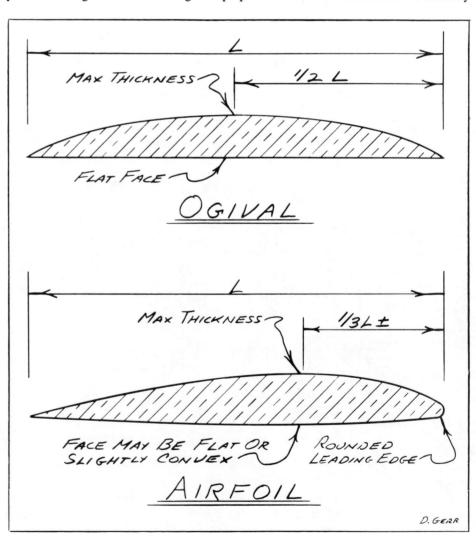

Figure 4-5

Ogival and airfoil blade sections.

determined shape that can dramatically affect performance. The two most common shapes for cross-sections through a propeller blade are *ogival* and *airfoil*. An *ogival* or *flat-faced* blade is made with its face dead flat—as expanded—and its back symmetrically rounded. The leading and trailing edges of the blade are usually as sharp as possible, consistent with strength. The back or suction surface is rounded in a perfect circular segment, an ellipse, or a sine curve, with the maximum height or blade thickness exactly at the midpoint of blade width.

Airfoil blade sections resemble traditional airplane wing sections. The leading edge is rounded—not sharp—and the maximum blade thickness, or *chord*, usually occurs about a third of the blade width aft of the leading edge. The blade face is generally flat, though some airfoil blades have a small amount of convexity to their faces.

Effects of Blade Section Shape Since propeller blades generate thrust by producing lift—very much like airplane wings—you might expect that most propeller sections would have an airfoil shape. Interestingly, this is generally not the case. The suction surface of an airfoil blade actually generates too much lift, creating local areas—just

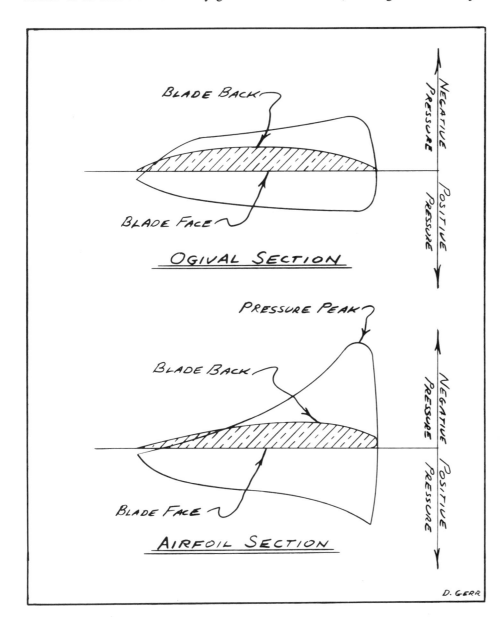

Figure 4-6

Pressures on ogival and airfoil section blades.

behind the leading edge—of very large negative pressure (suction). This leads to early cavitation (see later sections in this chapter). To avoid this, most propellers use the ogival shape.

In many modern propellers, a small amount of airfoil section is worked into the blades at the root. This is because the actual speed through the water of the inner parts of the blade is substantially slower than for the sections at the tip. Thus, the inner parts of the blade can safely be made to generate a bit of additional lift without creating excessive negative pressure and cavitation.

Following such blades out from the root, the airfoil section gradually disappears until—at 55 to 70 percent of the blade length out from the hub—the blades return to completely ogival section. Although such blades can increase performance, the gains are usually small—in the region of a 3- or 4-percent increase in efficiency. Since entirely ogival blades are easier and less expensive to produce, manufacturers continue to offer them, and they are more than satisfactory for most installations.

Blade-Thickness Fraction (BTF) or Axial-Thickness Ratio

Blade thickness is usually defined in terms of *blade-thickness fraction* or *axial-thickness ratio,* which is the maximum thickness of the blade divided by its diameter. Since a blade gets thinner as it progresses from root to tip, the maximum thickness is taken at an imaginary point on the shaft centerline. The line of the blade face is extended down to intersect with the shaft centerline at point O, and the line of the blade back is extended to point A on the shaft centerline. The distance $\overline{OA}$ or t_0 divided by the diameter equals the *blade-thickness fraction.* Blade-thickness fractions for average propellers usually fall between 0.04 and 0.06 (see Figure 4-11).

Formula 4-8   Blade-Thickness Fraction Formula

Formula 4-8

$BTF = t_0 \div D$
Where:
BTF = Blade-thickness fraction
D = Diameter
t_0 = Maximum blade thickness as extended to shaft centerline

Effects of Blade Thickness   All other things being equal, a thinner blade is more efficient than a fatter, thicker one. There must, however, be enough thickness to create the desired sectional shape. In addition, blade thickness must be large enough to generate sufficient strength—if blades are too thin, they will break under extreme loading. A rough rule of thumb is that the blade thickness fraction should equal 16 percent of the mean-width ratio (MWR). Accordingly, a standard propeller with a MWR of 0.33 would have a BTF of about 0.053 **[0.33 MWR × 0.16 = 0.053]**.

In order to keep highly loaded, high-RPM propeller blades from becoming excessively thick and losing efficiency, high-strength alloys are frequently used—particularly in waters where there is substantial chance of hitting floating debris. Manganese bronze is actually a type of brass commonly used for average propellers, though vulnerable to corrosion. Stainless steel is used for propellers under high load, and Nibral or NAB (an alloy of nickel, bronze and aluminum), and also aluminum bronze, are indicated for applications requiring extreme strength and good corrosion resistance.

Blade Contour

The shape of the blades as viewed from astern is their *contour.* Average propeller blades are narrowest at the root and broadest about 50 to 66 percent of the radius out from the centerline. Such blades generally have maximum widths between 25 and 40 percent of their diameters.

The amount of blade area that can be driven by a given horsepower and diameter is limited, so area is distributed where it will do the most good. Since the tips of the blades are traveling the greatest distance, they can do the most work. Thus, the natural tendency is to try to get all the blade area as far out as possible. Obviously, the propeller cannot have tiny shafts supporting huge plates at the tips, so we compromise on the elliptical shape that is most common. That way the root is strong enough to support the loads on the middle and tip, while the outer part of the blade is not so big that it gets in the way of the water going to the blade behind it or bends excessively.

Very slow-turning propellers customarily have their blade areas distributed farther out, with the maximum blade width occurring at as much as 75 percent of the radius. Propellers with four, five, or more blades frequently have long, narrow blades of low mean-width ratio to reduce total blade area.

Effects of Blade Contour   Blade contour is very closely related to blade width. Since most blades are roughly elliptical in contour, squatter, broader contours are associated with wide blades or blades of high mean-width ratio. The comments on the effects of blade width apply here, too.

Skew

When the contour of the blade is not symmetrical but swept back, the blade is said to have *skew* or *skew back*. Moderate-speed propellers usually have little or no skew, while medium- to high-speed propellers will have a small amount of skew back.

Effects of Skew   Skew causes radial sections of the blades to enter the water sequentially, instead of all at roughly the same time. This can help reduce vibration, especially at high RPMs, by easing the transition of the blades from the full slipstream to the much slower

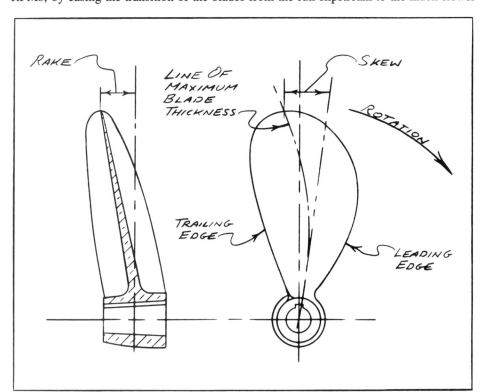

Figure 4-7

Blade with skew and rake.

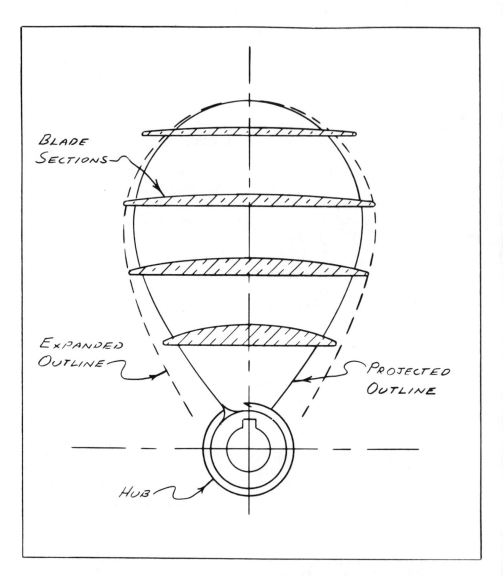

Figure 4-8

Standard ogival section blade without skew.

slipstream in the shadow of the deadwood or strut. Where vibration is a problem, you can switch to a moderately skewed propeller of similar dimensions with little sacrifice in thrust.

Pronounced skew is usually seen on weedless or non-fouling propellers. Although these propellers have noticeably less efficiency than less skewed propellers, in weed-infested waters, freedom from fouling more than pays back this loss. Specialized propellers for large, high-speed craft, such as destroyers or sub-chasers, may show pronounced skew back to compensate for radial differences in the water flow to the propeller blades as a result of hull interference, and to decrease propeller noise. These types of propellers, however, require detailed computer analysis and tank testing and are beyond the scope of this book.

Rake and Rake Ratio

When the propeller blades lean or slope either forward or aft as viewed from the side they are said to have *rake*. Blades that slope aft have *positive rake*, while blades that slope forward have *negative rake*. Rake is indicated either as a slope in degrees, or by *rake ratio*. The rake ratio is defined as shown in Figure 4-11. A vertical line from the tip of the blade is dropped to intersect with the shaft centerline at point B, and the face of the blade is extended to meet the shaft centerline at point O. The distance $\overline{BO}$ divided by diameter is the rake ratio. When B falls directly on O, the blades are vertical (have no rake).

Formula 4-9   Rake Ratio Formula

Rake ratio $= \overline{BO} \div D$

Where:

$\overline{BO}$ = distance between tip of blade projected down to the shaft centerline and face of blade extended down to shaft centerline

D = diameter

Formula 4-9

Effects of Rake   For almost all normal applications vertical blades are optimum. Blades raked aft are chiefly used to steal a bit of additional effective diameter in tight situations. This is because the raked blades have more length and thus more area than vertical blades of the same diameter. In addition, the raked blades, whose tips end farther aft, can take advantage of the fact that the hull sweeps up slightly, permitting a somewhat greater propeller diameter. Blades with negative rake are usually found on extremely high-speed vessels and highly loaded propellers. In these conditions, the rake can help strengthen the blades.

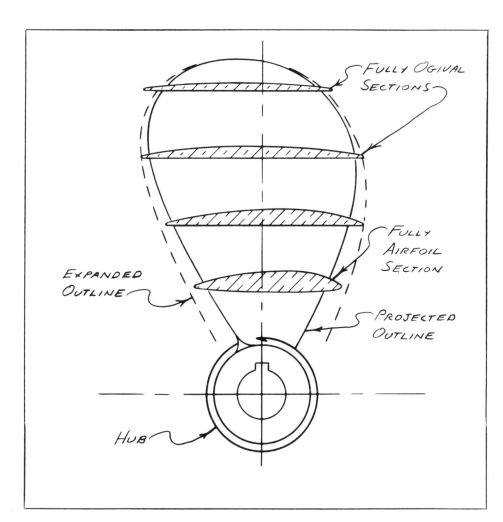

Figure 4-9

Blade with airfoil section at root, returning to fully ogival section at 40% diameter, and with moderate skew.

Figure 4-10

A three-bladed propeller with moderately skewed blades. The mean-width ratio of the blades is 0.33 and the disc-area ratio is 0.55. These propellers are best suited to use on moderate- to moderately high-speed craft such as yachts, fast commuters, light, fast fishing vessels, and so on. For vessels operating over 35 knots, this pattern is available with cupped blades.

(Courtesy of The Michigan Wheel Company)

Cupped Blades

Cupped blades are blades with hollow or concave faces. There are many variations of blade cup, but the most common is to introduce cup at the trailing edge. Sometimes, this cupping is worked around and into part of the blade tip as well.

Effects of Blade Cup Cupped blades have the effect of increasing true or virtual pitch. A good rule of thumb is to select blades with 1 inch or 5 percent less pitch than a similar uncupped blade. Cupped blades are very effective on high-speed vessels (over 35 knots), particularly with high-RPM propellers. For such craft, cupped-bladed propellers can produce speed increases of as much as 6 to 12 percent. On a 40-knot vessel, this would work out to approximately 3.6 knots.

Cupped blades also help delay or reduce cavitation, which is always a potential problem in high-speed and highly loaded propellers. Further, the curvature created by the cup imparts additional strength to the blade, allowing for thinner blades and, again, higher

Figure 4-11

Rake ratio and thickness fraction.

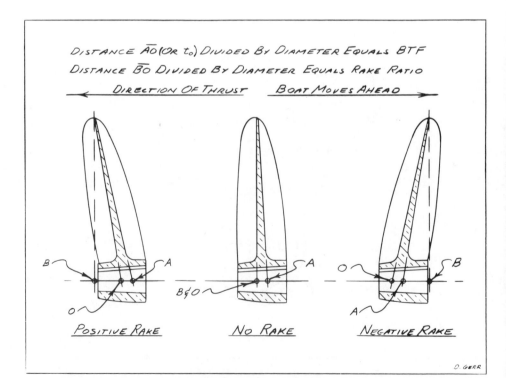

efficiency at high speeds. In spite of the many advantages cupped blades can offer high-speed craft, they serve no useful function on most vessels operating at under 30 knots.

CAVITATION

Cavitation is bubbles of partial vacuum caused by excessive propeller speed or loading. To avoid this condition, the negative pressure on the blade back (the suction face) must remain less than the local (ambient) pressure of the water at the propeller. For most installations the ambient pressure is equal to the pressure of the atmosphere at sea level, about 14.7 pounds per square inch (101326 N/m²), plus the pressure generated by the head of water above the propeller and minus the vapor pressure of the water. On average vessels this comes to around 13.9 PSI. Thus, if the lift or suction on any portion of the blade back exceeds 14 PSI, cavitation is very likely to occur.

High-RPM airfoil sections that produce negative pressure peaks, large amounts of *slip* (see next chapter), excessive pitch, and high tip speeds all tend to create or increase cavitation. Thus, cavitation is seldom a problem on low-speed vessels with slow RPMs. Keeping RPMs down, using ogival section blades (particularly at the tips), decreasing pitch slightly at the blade tips, and keeping pitch ratios as low as possible all help eliminate or reduce cavitation.

Effects of Cavitation

Contrary to what most people think, cavitating propellers can still generate plenty of thrust. The problem is that the vacuum bubbles implode against the propeller, causing vibration and pitting. The vacuum bubbles form and implode irregularly, causing uneven pressure both along the blades and between them. This creates vibration identical to having unbalanced or unequally pitched blades. What's more, the force of the imploding bubbles is so great that it actually sucks metal right off the surface of the propeller. The resultant pitting leads to uneven wear, bad balance and even more vibration.

Supercavitating and Fully Cavitating Propellers

Vessels operating at high speeds (over 35 knots) and at high shaft RPMs are frequently forced into operating regimes in which cavitation is difficult to avoid. One solution is to use *supercavitating* or *fully cavitating* propellers, specifically designed to operate during cavitation. Even though supercavitating propellers are not generally quite as efficient as standard noncavitating propellers, practical limitations on propeller diameter and RPM frequently make supercavitating propellers attractive options.

In order to avoid the pitting and vibration caused by cavitation, the blades on supercavitating propellers are shaped so the bubbles will not implode against them. Although there are a number of approaches to this, you can frequently recognize this sort of propeller by its scimitar-like blade shape.

VENTILATION

Ventilation is often confused with cavitation, though actually it is quite different. Whereas cavitation comprises actual regions of partial vacuum, ventilation is caused by the propeller's sucking air down from the water's surface. This is not usually as severe a problem as cavitation, but it can lead to vibration and loss of thrust. Some propellers, such as surface propellers, are specifically designed to work with air entrained in the wake, but for most propellers ventilation should be avoided. The best way to correct ventilation is to get the propeller deeper under the surface, which sometimes can be accomplished simply by reducing diameter. Using a propeller with blades raked aft is also helpful in reducing ventilation, since the force of water streaming out along the raked blades reduces the tendency of air to be pulled into the propeller disc.

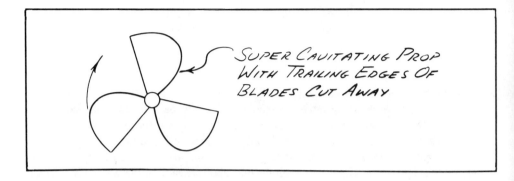

Figure 4-12

Supercavitating propeller.

SPECIAL TYPES OF PROPELLERS

Ducted Propellers

Ducted propellers or *kort nozzles* are surrounded with a closely fitted, circular shroud of airfoil section. The propeller blades are square-tipped, almost like standard elliptical blades with the outer 20 percent chopped off at right angles, with very little clearance between the blade tips and the inside of the shroud.

Effects of Ducted Propellers Ducted propellers can substantially increase the thrust generated by an engine of a given horsepower as compared with standard propellers. This effect is significant only on low-speed vessels such as tugs and trawlers that operate under 9 or 10 knots and have heavily loaded blades. In such applications, the expense and complication of installing a ducted propeller can be recouped in the ability to tow heavier loads at higher speeds. On most other vessels, the ducted propeller offers little if any advantage to compensate for its additional cost. We will investigate ducted propellers in more detail in Chapter 8.

Surface Propellers

Surface propellers are designed to operate roughly half in and half out of the water. This would lead one to expect that surface propellers would cavitate all the time, but just the opposite is the case. Since every blade is exposed to the air once each revolution, the surface propeller is actually fully aerated. Since cavitation is vacuum, the aeration prevents cavitation from occurring.

Effects of Surface Propellers Surface propellers are in effect efficient, noncavitating propellers that can operate at high RPM on high-speed boats without cavitation problems. These propellers are only useful on vessels that operate regularly over 35 knots, with substantial gains appearing only at speeds over 40 knots. Originally, surface propellers were installed on fixed shafts projecting beyond the transom, and vessels equipped with them were steered with ordinary rudders situated well aft. Many modern installations place the surface propeller on an articulated shaft that allows steering like an outdrive, thus eliminating the rudder.

Such installations permit the ultimate in reduction of appendage resistance. Not only is there no rudder and no shaft strut ahead of the propeller, but only a portion of the propeller shaft and propeller is in the water. Some surface propeller installations also allow the operator to pivot the shaft up and down, as well as from side to side. Although this has little effect on boat trim, it effectively allows the operator to have a variable-diameter propeller, which is very useful in adjusting thrust and power absorption. We will discuss surface propellers further in Chapter 9.

RULES OF THUMB

There are countless rules of thumb floating around about propellers. Some are useful and some are worthless. We will take a brief look at a few of them.

1. *One inch in diameter absorbs the torque of two to three inches of pitch.* This is a good rough guide. Both pitch and diameter absorb the torque generated by the engine. Diameter is, by far, the most important factor. Thus, the ratio of 2 to 3 inches of pitch equals 1 inch in diameter is a fair guide. It is no more than that, however. You could not select a suitable propeller based only on this rule.

2. *The higher the pitch your engine can turn near top horsepower and RPM, the faster your boat can go.* This is also accurate as far as it goes. The greater the pitch, the greater the distance your boat will advance each revolution. Since top engine RPM is constant, increasing pitch means more speed. Then, why aren't all propellers as small in diameter as possible, with gigantic pitches?

   The answer is simply that when the pitch gets too large, the angle of attack of the propeller blades to the onrushing water becomes too steep and they stall. This is exactly the same as an airplane wing's stalling in too steep a climb. The pitches and pitch ratios we explore in Chapters 5 and 6 are optimum. Within these limits it is worthwhile, on high-speed craft, to use the smallest diameter and the greatest pitch possible.

3. *Too little pitch can ruin an engine.* This is quite true if the pitch and diameter combined are so low that it allows the engine to race at speeds far over its designed top-rated RPM. Never allow your engine to operate at more than 103 to 105 percent of top-rated RPM. If your engine exceeds that figure, a propeller with increased pitch or diameter is indicated.

4. *Every two-inch increase in pitch will decrease engine speed by 450 RPM, and vice versa.* This is a good rough guide for moderate- to high-speed pleasure craft, passenger vessels and crew boats. Like all rules of thumb, though, it is no more than a rough guide.

5. *A square wheel (a propeller with exactly the same diameter and pitch) is the most efficient.* This is not true. There is nothing wrong with a square wheel; on the other hand, there is nothing special about it, either.

6. *The same propeller can't deliver both high speed and maximum power.* This is true. A propeller sized for high speed has a small diameter and maximum pitch. A propeller sized for power or thrust has a large diameter. For some boats you can compromise on an in-between propeller, but for either real speed or real thrust there is little common ground.

Chapter 5
Crouch's Propeller Method
The Empirical Method for Calculating Propellers Using Slip

$\mathbf{F}$or many years engineers have used the analogy of a wood screw in soft pine to explain propeller operation. This analogy is so intuitive and has persisted for so long that many propeller terms, including the terms *screw propeller* and *pitch,* are based on this assumption. In fact, in its best form, this analogy is still used by some designers, as embodied by the tables and formulas developed and refined largely by George Crouch.

Because it is so intuitive and because it is the "traditional" method of propeller calculation, we will examine the Crouch or slip method first. I recommend, however, that the Bp-δ method (pronounced "bee pee delta"), which we'll cover in the next chapter, be used for final calculations when precision is needed. Most modern propeller experts use the Crouch method only for rough estimates, relying on the Bp-δ or other more mathematically exact methods for installations demanding efficiency. The slip method is perfectly adequate, however, when peak efficiency is not important, as for example in auxiliary sailboats.

A propeller must meet two completely different requirements: it must match the boat's hull, and it must match its engine. In Chapters 1 and 2 we discussed the selection of a suitable engine and what speed we can expect the vessel to obtain with that engine. Now that we have learned how a propeller's shape is defined, the question remains how to determine the correct propeller for a specific vessel.

DETERMINING SLIP AND PITCH

Matching Pitch to Speed

A hull requires a certain amount of thrust to push it forward, and we need to pick a propeller that will generate as much thrust as possible at the intended operating speed. Let us take, for example, *Svelte Samantha,* a single-screw cabin cruiser intended to cruise at 18 knots (a SL ratio of 3.3), at 75 percent of full engine RPMs—she will have a typical light, high-speed engine. With this information, we can start to calculate the proper propeller pitch. Our aim is to have the propeller advance the same distance the boat will at speed. *Svelte Samantha*'s characteristics are as follows:

Svelte Samantha		
34 ft.	10.36 m	LOA (length overall)
30 ft.	9.14 m	WL (waterline length)
11 ft.	3.35 m	BOA (beam overall)
10 ft.	3.05 m	BWL (waterline beam)
1.34 ft.	0.40 m	Hd (hull draft)
12,700 lb	5760 kg	Displacement
18 kt	18 kt	Desired cruising speed

Using Formula 2-4, we determine that *Svelte Samantha* requires 182 SHP (136 kw) at the propeller to achieve 18 knots (using a C of 150, for an average cruiser). Accordingly, *Svelte Samantha*'s engine should be rated 240 BHP (197 kw) [**182 Hp ÷ 0.75 = 242 HP**], and the engine chosen delivers this at 3,000 RPM, with a 2.4-to-1 reduction gear. This means that *Samantha*'s propeller will turn at 1,250 RPMs with the throttle wide open [**3,000 RPM ÷ 2.4 = 1,250 RPM**].

Determining Which RPM to Use in Finding Pitch

Here, we face an important compromise. We found in Chapters 1 and 2 that cruising speed should be at 70 to 85 percent of top rated engine RPM (as is the case with *Svelte Samantha*). Since our propeller will be of fixed pitch, however, if it is pitched for ideal operation at 75-percent RPM, it will be way off at full RPM. A good average is to base pitch on operation at 90 percent of maximum RPM, which will yield about 90 percent of the maximum SHP. For *Svelte Samantha,* this works out to a shaft speed of 1,125 RPM at around 216 SHP (161 kw). Our cruising speed will be a bit below this, but we will still be able to open the throttle up to get top revolutions when needed. We must now base our pitch calculation on speed at 90 percent of full throttle. Two hundred and sixteen SHP yields 58.8 pounds per horsepower (35.7 kg per kw). Formula 2-4 gives a V of 19.5 knots.

Figuring Pitch Without Slip

Once we know our speed, all we have to do is find the pitch that will give us the same forward distance traveled per minute as the boat will go at 19.5 knots. Since we know the boat speed in nautical miles per hour (knots) and the propeller pitch in inches and RPM, we have to find some common ground—in this case, feet per minute. To convert knots to feet per minute, multiply by 101.3 (to convert miles per hour to feet per minute, multiply by 88). Thus, *Svelte Samantha* is moving along at a V of 1,975.3 feet per minute [**19.5 knots × 101.3 = 1,975.3 ft./min.**]. Our propeller is turning at 1,125 RPMs. If we divide *Samantha*'s speed of 1.975.3 feet per minute by 1,125 RPMs, we find that our propeller should have a pitch of 1.75 feet (0.53 m) [**1.975.3 ft./min. ÷ 1,125 RPMs = 1.75 ft.**]. Since propeller pitches are usually specified in inches, we multiply 1.75 feet by 12 and find that *Svelte Samantha* requires a propeller with a 21-inch (533 mm) pitch.

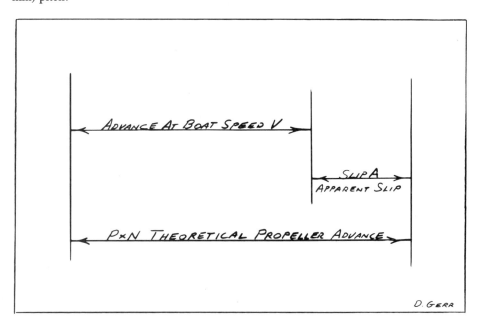

Figure 5-1

Apparent slip.

Slip

In reality, water is not like soft pine. It's a fluid and so a propeller *slips* or slides a bit as it rotates. It's more exact to view slip as the difference between the distance a boat actually travels through the water—in the time of one complete propeller revolution at her speed through the water, V—and the theoretical distance it would travel if it advanced the full pitch of the propeller (see Figure 5–1). This difference is called *apparent slip* (SlipA) and is expressed as a percent of theoretical propeller advance (pitch times RPM).

The only way to find slip exactly is to take a boat out and run her on a measured mile. Carefully timing the runs gives the exact speed and, knowing RPM and pitch, you can use the above relationship with the following formula to find slip:

Formula 5-1 Apparent Slip Formula

$$\text{SlipA} = \frac{(P/12 \times RPM) - (Kts \times 101.3)}{(P/12 \times RPM)}$$

Which may be conveniently restated as:

Formula 5-1

$$P = \frac{Kts \times 1215.6}{RPM \times (1 - SlipA)}$$

Where:

SlipA = Apparent slip

P = Propeller face pitch in inches

Kts = Boat speed through water or V in knots

RPM = Revolutions per minute of the propeller

CHART 5-1 SLIP VS PITCH

A

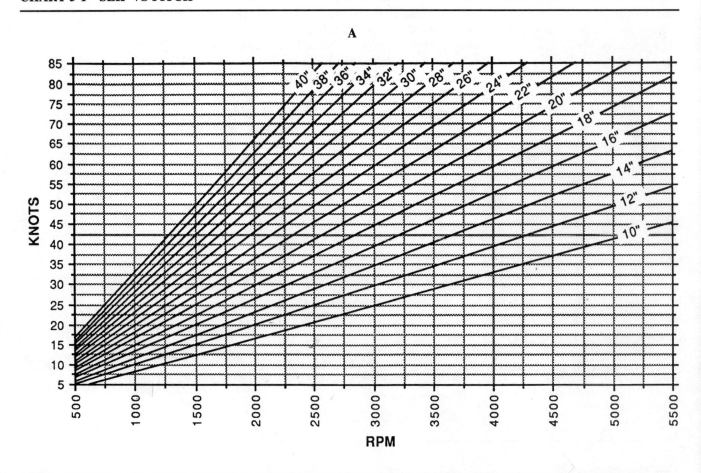

B

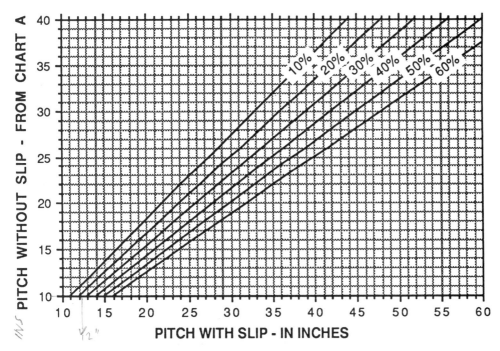

Chart 5-1A and B. *These charts, related to Formula 5-1, may be used in two ways. In the first, apparent slip can be estimated from the results of a timed run over a measured mile. Enter Chart A with the measured speed and RPM, and read off the "pitch without slip." Enter Chart B with this value and your propeller's actual known pitch, and read out the apparent slip as a percent of theoretical propeller advance (pitch times RPM). The second, more common use of the charts is to calculate the needed propeller pitch for a new boat design or a repowering, using the desired speed and RPM and an estimated value for slip. Again, read out a value for "pitch without slip" from Chart A. Then enter Chart B with this value and a slip estimate from Chart 5-2 or Table 5-1.*

It is important to run a course between fixed points as specified on a proper navigation chart. Obviously, using a "measured mile" that was not an exact mile would throw your calculations completely off. Bear in mind that buoys can drag sufficiently to throw off their locations. In addition, the mile should be run at least twice, in opposite directions, and the results averaged to cancel out the effects of wind and current. For really accurate work, run the course both ways three times. Since we are dealing with a new design, a repowering or a new propeller, we have to estimate slip. This is the chief drawback to the slip method of finding pitch. There is no precise way to determine slip short of putting a propeller on a boat and running a measured mile.

Estimating Slip for Finding Pitch

Chart 5-2 plots slip as a function of boat speed in knots. It is based on the formula:

Formula 5-2   Slip vs Boat Speed Formula

SLIP $= 1.4 \div Kts^{0.57}$

Where:

Kts $=$ Boat speed in knots

This formula was derived by the author, and checks very well against known slip values from a wide variety of sources. [Note: Appendix D provides a quick math review for those who are unfamiliar with or rusty on decimal exponents.]

Formula 5-2

CHART 5-2 SLIP VS BOAT SPEED

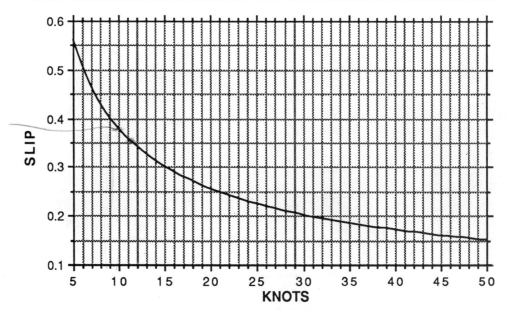

Chart 5-2. *This chart, constructed from Formula 5-2, shows slip as a function of speed. This empirical relationship, derived by the author, checks well against known values.*

The results from Formula 5-2 should be averaged against the information in Table 5-1 to see if the slip value makes sense for the type of vessel being considered.

TABLE 5-1 TYPICAL SLIP VALUES

TABLE 5-1

Type of Boat	Speed in Knots	Percent of Slip
Auxiliary sailboats, barges	under 9	45%
Heavy powerboats, workboats	9–15	26%
Lightweight powerboats, cruisers	15–30	24%
High-speed planing boats	30–45	20%
Planing race boats, vee-bottom	45–90	10%
Stepped hydroplanes, catamarans	over 90	7%

Slip and Efficiency Are Not the Same

People frequently mistake slip (SlipA) for efficiency, abbreviated as *e* or η (the Greek letter E, pronounced "eta"), and thus try to eliminate it altogether. Actually the two concepts are quite different—although they are very closely related. (See Efficiency vs Slip Chart 5-6.) Slip, in fact, is actually *required* to produce thrust. Though it's a good practice to keep slip fairly low, the slip values given in Table 5-1 are close to optimum. You cannot eliminate slip and would not want to if you could, for then you would have no thrust at all.

Finding Pitch with Slip

Using Chart 5-2 or Formula 5-2, we find a slip for *Svelte Samantha* of 27 percent. Let's check against the Table 5-1, Typical Slip Values. *Svelte Samantha* is a light cabin cruiser. With her accommodations, she is a bit heavier than a lightweight powerboat. The table indicates a slip of 25 percent or so. Accordingly, we will compromise on a 26-percent slip. The next step is simply to increase the 21.1-inch (533 mm) pitch we derived earlier (the pitch without slip) by 26 percent to get a 26.5-inch (673 mm) pitch [**1.26 × 21.1 in. = 26.58 in.**]. (Pitches should be rounded down unless the decimal is 0.7 or greater.)

Slip vs Pitch Chart 5-1 plots pitch against RPM and speed (V), in knots, for various apparent slips. It is based on the SlipA (apparent slip) calculations (Formula 5-1) given above. To use this chart, enter speed and RPM on Chart 5-1A and find the pitch without slip. Next, obtain a suitable slip value from Chart 5-2 or Formula 5-2 and Table 5-1. Pitch may then be read directly from Chart 5-1B, or pitch may be calculated directly using Formula 5-1.

DETERMINING DIAMETER

Factors Controlling Diameter

We must now determine a suitable diameter. Two major factors control propeller diameter—engine horsepower in relation to shaft RPM, and hull resistance. Except for high-speed craft, a larger-diameter propeller is always more efficient than a smaller one. In other words, you will get more thrust or push with the same engine and a larger-diameter propeller. Obviously, you cannot have a propeller as big as a helicopter rotor. Not only are there practical restrictions due to draft and hull shape, but your engine would never have enough power to move it through something as dense as seawater, no matter how slowly.

The key here, though, is that the slower the RPM, the larger the diameter an engine can turn. As we discussed in Chapters 1 and 2, shaft speed, not engine speed, is the important thing. The reduction gear ratio is critical here. The greater the reduction, the slower the shaft speed and the bigger the propeller can be, within the boat's draft and hull shape limitations.

Determining RPM for Calculating Diameter

When calculating pitch, we compromised and used 90 percent of SHP and RPM. In determining diameter, however, we must use 100 percent of full RPM or very close to that. This is because diameter is the most important factor in determining the amount of power a propeller absorbs. If we were to base our diameter calculation on an RPM figure much lower than the engine's maximum, we would be holding engine RPM down. (It would not have enough power to turn the large propeller at full RPM.) This would limit both boat speed and engine speed, and can damage the engine. Accordingly, for light- to moderate-weight vessels such as yachts, high-speed utility boats and light passenger vessels, diameter should be calculated at 100 percent of top RPM and SHP. This is, in effect, ensuring that the propeller power curve crosses the engine power curve at the latter's maximum, as discussed in Chapter 1.

For heavier workboats, where maximum thrust and efficiency at cruising speed is more important than getting top speed when the throttle is opened wide, diameter may be calculated based on 95 to 98 percent of engine RPM. This will cause the propeller power curve (see Chapter 1) to cross the engine power curve just below the maximum. Holding the engine RPM down in this way is not harmful, and the larger diameter that may be obtained increases efficiency at cruising speed. The penalty, though, is that top boat speed (V) will be decreased slightly.

Finding Diameter From HP and RPM

Diameter-HP-RPM Charts 5-3A, B, C, and D plot diameter against SHP and RPM at the propeller. They are based on three-bladed propellers of standard elliptical contour and ogival (flat-faced) section, with blade widths of about a 0.33 mean-width ratio. This propeller type will be found to give good results for almost all ordinary installations.

The curves in Chart 5-3 are based on the formula:

Formula 5-3   DIA-HP-RPM Formula

Formula 5-3

$$D = \frac{632.7 \times SHP^{0.2}}{RPM^{0.6}}$$

Where:

D = Propeller diameter in inches

SHP = Shaft horsepower at the propeller

RPM = Shaft RPM at the propeller

CHART 5-3   DIAMETER - HP - RPM CHARTS

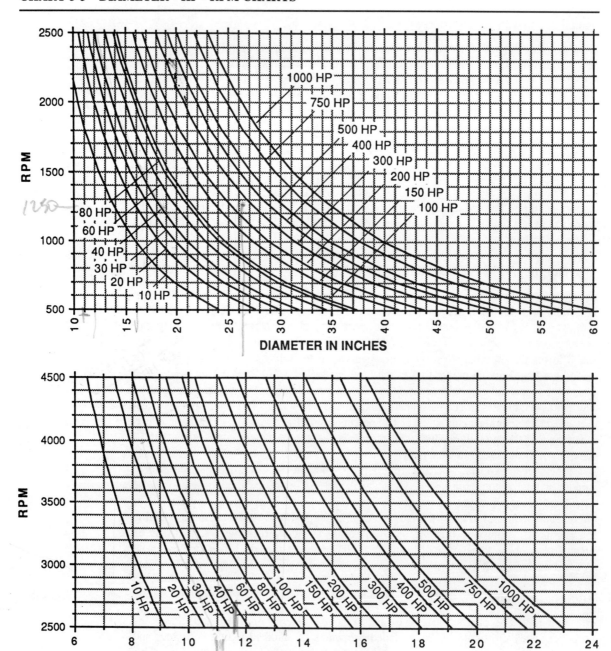

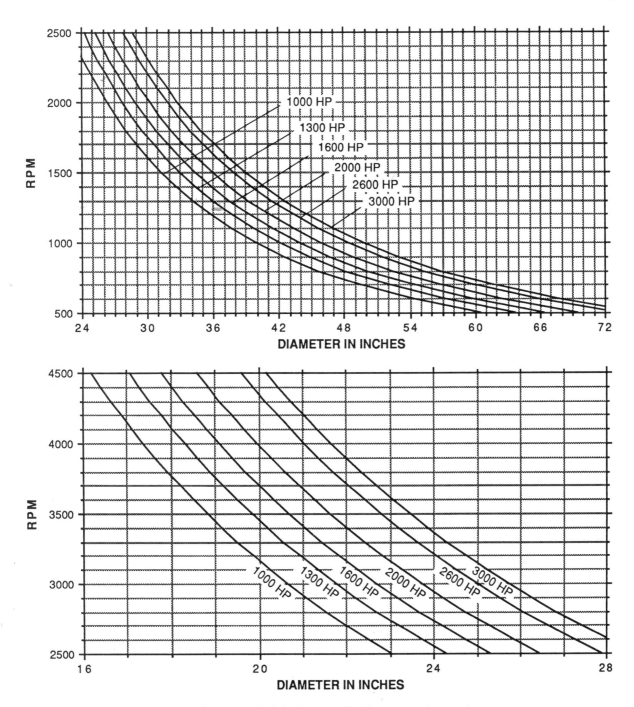

Chart 5-3. *These charts, derived from Formula 5-3, plot propeller diameter against maximum rated shaft horsepower and RPM at the propeller, and can be applied to most installations.*

Based on 100 percent of RPM and SHP, Chart 5–3 or Formula 5–3 shows that *Svelte Samantha*'s engine, delivering 240 SHP (180 kw), can turn a 26.2-inch (673 mm) propeller at 1,250 RPM. Accordingly, a 26.2-inch-diameter propeller with a 26.5-inch pitch (665 mm by 673 mm) would do the job. In the U.S., stock propellers are manufactured in one-inch increments up to 36-inch diameters, and in two-inch increments in sizes larger than 36 inches. Thus, we would specify 26 inches (660 mm) for each measurement. This just happens to work out to be a square wheel (pitch ratio of 1).

TWO- AND FOUR-BLADED PROPELLERS

Adjusting Diameter and Pitch for 2- and 4-Bladed Propellers

To find diameter and pitch for two- and four-bladed propellers, we multiply the dimensions for the standard three-bladed propeller by the following quantities:

TABLE 5-2

TABLE 5-2   TWO- AND FOUR-BLADED CONVERSION FACTORS

	Diameter	Pitch	Efficiency
Two-Bladed Propeller	1.05	1.01	1.02
Four-Bladed Propeller	0.94	0.98	0.96

Accordingly, if we wished to install a four-bladed propeller on *Svelte Samantha*, we would use a 24-inch-diameter by 25-inch-pitch propeller (610 mm by 635 mm) [**26 in. dia. × 0.94 = 24.4 in. dia., and 26 in. pitch × 0.98 = 25.48 in. pitch**]. Note that the efficiency (e) or (η) of the four-bladed propeller would be only 96 percent of the three-blader. This will not actually affect cruising speed. Since we had originally planned on cruising at 75 percent of top RPM, we would now operate at around 78 percent of top RPM, which is acceptable. Top speed potential will drop off slightly, however. In return for this, the four-bladed propeller will have smoother operation, with noticeably less vibration.

Interestingly, a two-bladed propeller of 5 percent greater diameter (27 inches) would be 2 percent more efficient than the standard three-bladed propeller. Drawbacks, though, are that the two-bladed propeller could have noticeably more vibration than the three-blader, and the reduced blade area may cause cavitation as well.

CHECKING PITCH RATIO AND MINIMUM DIAMETER

Checking for Optimum Pitch Ratio

Let's now check to see that the pitch ratio of the propeller we've selected is suitable for the type of vessel and speed we are considering.

Chart 5-4 gives optimum pitch-to-diameter ratios plotted against boat speed (V), in knots. These curves are based on the following formulas:

Optimum Pitch Ratio Formulas

Formula 5-4a,b,c

    Formula 5-4a
    Average Pitch Ratio $= 0.46 \times Kts^{0.26}$
    Formula 5-4b
    Maximum Pitch Ratio $= 0.52 \times Kts^{0.28}$
    Formula 5-4c
    Minimum Pitch Ratio $= 0.39 \times Kts^{0.23}$
    These formulas were derived by the author and have been found to check well with a wide
    variety of vessels.

Generally, the best performance and efficiency will be obtained with pitch ratios close to the average pitch ratio curve (see Formula 5-4a). Performance will be satisfactory, however, as long as the pitch ratio of the specified propeller does not fall above or below the recommended maximum or minimum curves. If the pitch ratio does fall outside these curves, the shaft speed is unsuited to the boat and must be changed using either a different reduction gear and/or an engine of a different rated RPM.

Propellers on twin-screw craft tend to have higher pitch ratios than single-screw vessels since the individual propeller diameters are smaller, but the craft is still advancing at the

CHART 5-4 OPTIMUM PITCH RATIO

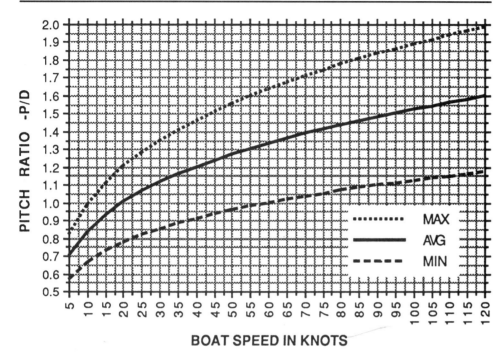

Chart 5-4. *The relationship between optimum pitch-to-diameter ratios and boat speed in knots. Related to Formulas 5-4a, b, and c.*

same speed as a comparable single-screw vessel. Thus, pitch remains the same, or nearly the same, as with the single-screw version.

For *Svelte Samantha*, whose speed at the designed pitch is 19.5 knots, the average pitch ratio curve (see Chart 5-4 or Formula 5-4a) gives a recommended pitch ratio of 0.99. This is virtually identical to our specified pitch ratio of 1, so this pitch ratio is suitable.

Determining Minimum Acceptable Diameter

It is also important to make sure that the propeller diameter specified matches the hull. A very small propeller turning at high RPM can offer adequate performance at full speed, but it will not provide sufficient thrust at low speed, while getting up onto a plane, or during maneuvering.

Minimum Diameter Chart 5-5 plots the minimum propeller diameter required for useful thrust at all speeds, for both single- and twin-screw vessels. Propellers with smaller diameters than those given in Chart 5-5 should be avoided. The curves are based on the following formula:

Formula 5-5 *Minimum Diameter Formula*

$D_{min} = 4.07 \times (BWL \times H_d)^{0.5}$

Where:

D_{min} = Minimum acceptable propeller diameter in inches

BWL = Beam on the waterline in feet

H_d = Draft of hull from the waterline down (excluding keel, skeg or deadwood) in feet

(Hull draft is the depth of the hull body to the fairbody line, rabbet, or the hull's intersection with the top of the keel. It thus excludes keel and/or skeg.)

D_{min} for Twin Screws = $0.8 \times D_{min}$

D_{min} for Triple Screws = $0.65 \times D_{min}$

Formula 5-5

CHART 5-5   MINIMUM DIAMETER

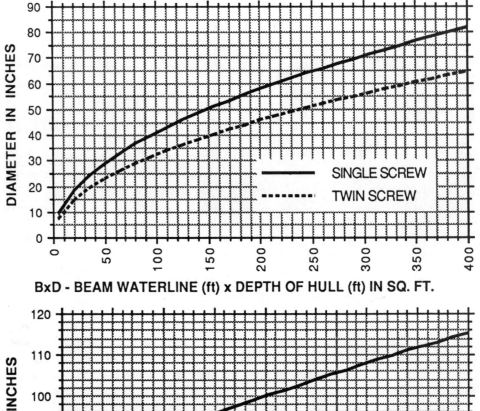

BxD - BEAM WATERLINE (ft) x DEPTH OF HULL (ft) IN SQ. FT.

Chart 5-5. *Minimum propeller diameter required for useful thrust at all speeds. Based on Formula 5-5.*

In the case of *Svelte Samantha,* this works out as follows: *Svelte Samantha* has a 10-foot (3.05 m) waterline beam and a 1 foot 4 inch (0.4 m) hull draft. Accordingly, from Chart 5-5 or Formula 5-5, her minimum propeller diameter is 14.9 inches (378 mm) [**10 ft. × 1.34 ft. = 13.4 sq. ft., $\sqrt{13.4}$ = 3.66 in., and 3.66 × 4.07 = 14.9**]. We have already seen that *Samantha*'s engine and reduction gear combination can turn a 26-inch-diameter (660 mm) propeller, so we have no problem here—with diameter (at low and moderate speeds), bigger is better.

If the propeller we came up with had been smaller than the minimum diameter from Chart 5-5, we would have had to return to the beginning of our selection process and try a larger reduction gear and/or a slower-turning engine to allow an appropriate increase in diameter.

CHECKING FOR CAVITATION

Cavitation Formulas Can Be Complex and Contradictory

The final check we must make is for cavitation. As we discussed in Chapter 4, cavitation is vacuum bubbles caused by excessive blade loading. There are many methods of checking for the onset of cavitation, but most are excessively complex for use by small-craft designers, yard operators, boatbuilders, and boat owners. Not only that, but these complex methods frequently are no more accurate than simpler ones, since they don't allow for such factors as shaft inclination, strut and stern-bearing fairing, and so on, which can make two otherwise similar propellers behave quite differently, even at the same speed. Equally disconcerting is that two or three different methods of checking for cavitation can give two or three different results for the same propeller.

Finding Maximum Allowable Blade Loading

The clearest and most direct method of checking for cavitation is to determine blade loading or pressure in pounds per square inch (PSI). (In the metric system, this is expressed as newton meters squared, N/m^2, also called pascals, P.) Cavitation is a complex phenomenon and no single, simple formula can offer all the answers. The blade loading method that follows, however, is conservative, and thus generally safe as well as simple. The author has developed the following formula based on information from the tank tests at Wageningen and from Barnaby. It gives the pressure at which cavitation can be expected to occur.

Formula 5-6   Allowable Blade Loading Formula

$PSI = 1.9 \times Va^{0.5} \times Ft^{0.08}$

Where:

PSI = The pressure, in pounds per square inch, at which cavitation is likely to begin.

Va = The speed of water at the propeller (see next chapter regarding wake factor) in knots.

Ft = The depth of immersion of the propeller shaft centerline, during operation, in feet.

Formula 5-6

To check for cavitation we must use maximum speed, RPM and maximum SHP. For *Svelte Samantha,* with a 26-inch (660 mm) diameter propeller, we can assume that her shaft centerline will be just over a foot (0.36 m) below the surface. Her top speed at 240 HP (197 kw) as taken from Planing Speed Chart 2-3 or Formula 2-4 is 20.6 knots. The speed of water at the propeller is just slightly less than true boat speed for planing vessels (see next chapter regarding wake fraction). We can safely assume 96 percent of total boat speed, or 19.78 knots. Thus, the blade loading at which her propellers will start to cavitate works out as follows:

$PSI = 1.9 \times 19.78^{0.5} \times 1.2^{0.08}$

Therefore:

$PSI = 8.5$ (58600 N/m^2) for the onset of cavitation.

Determining Actual Blade Loading on a Propeller

We must now find the actual blade loading on *Svelte Samantha*'s propellers, as we have presently specified them. This is given by the following formula:

Formula 5-7   Actual Blade Loading Formula

Formula 5-7

$$PSI = \frac{326 \times SHP \times e}{Va \times Ad}$$

Where:

PSI = Blade loading in pounds per square inch.

SHP = Shaft horsepower at the propeller.

e = Propeller efficiency in open water.

Va = Speed of water at the propeller, in knots (see "Wake Fraction," next chapter).

Ad = Developed area of propeller blades, in square inches.

Before we can apply this formula we must have some estimate of the propeller's efficiency. When using the BP-δ method and the Taylor-Troost Bp-δ diagrams from the next chapter, this value can be read directly. Approximate Efficiency vs Slip Chart 5-6, however, plots approximate values of efficiency (e) or (η) relative to apparent slip (SlipA), for propellers of various pitch ratios. This chart is sufficiently accurate for the purpose of estimating blade pressure.

━━

CHART 5-6   APPROXIMATE EFFICIENCY VS SLIP

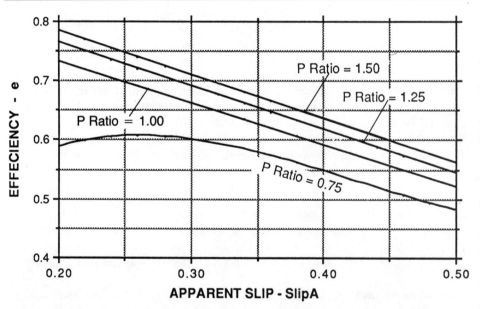

Chart 5-6. *Approximate efficiency relative to apparent slip for propellers of various pitch ratios.*

Entering Chart 5-6 with *Svelte Samantha*'s slip of 26 percent, and running up to her pitch ratio of 1, we get an efficiency of about 0.69. We can now calculate the blade loading on the 26-inch-diameter propeller of the 0.33 mean-width ratio that we have specified.

From Developed-Area Formula 4-7 or Chart 4-2, we find that a typical three-bladed propeller, 26 inches (660 mm) in diameter with a mean-width ratio of 0.33, has an expanded area of 268 square inches (1729 cm²). Accordingly:

$$PSI = \frac{326 \times 240\ SHP \times 0.69}{19.78\ Kts \times 268\ sq.\ in.}$$

Therefore:

PSI = 10.2 (70320 N/m²) blade loading.

━━

Adjusting Blade Width or MWR to Reduce Blade Loading

The 10.2 PSI figure we've derived using Formula 5-7 is 20 percent over the allowable loading of 8.5 PSI from Formula 5-6. Clearly, this propeller could experience some cavitation. Generally, the best solution is simply to specify a propeller of increased blade width or mean width ratio (MWR). Entering a 20-percent-larger MWR of 0.4 in Formula 4-7 or Chart 4-2 gives a developed area of 324 square inches (2090 cm²). Substituting this we get:

$$PSI = \frac{326 \times 240 \text{ SHP} \times 0.69}{19.78 \text{ Kts} \times 324 \text{ sq. in.}}$$

Therefore:

PSI = 8.4 (57910 N/m²) blade loading, which is acceptable.

Note that 324 square inches (2090 cm²) of developed area will remain about the minimum acceptable for *Svelte Samantha*. Our speed requirement remains constant and thus horsepower must remain constant. Therefore, regardless of the propeller chosen, the only real variable in determining blade loading will be small changes in efficiency with changes in pitch ratio.

In theory, the 0.4-MWR propeller, with its greater area, will absorb slightly more power and thus hold RPM down and decrease efficiency. In practice, the difference is negligible (usually less than 4 percent) in mean-width ratios from 0.3 to 0.55 for two-, three- and four-bladed propellers. (See Table 6-3 for exact values.)

Increasing the Number of Blades to Reduce Blade Loading

Another alternative for increasing area to reduce cavitation is simply to substitute a four-bladed propeller of the same pattern as the three-blader. We can try this with *Svelte Samantha*'s propeller. Earlier, we determined that we would use a 24-inch-diameter by 25-inch-pitch (609 mm by 635 mm) four-bladed propeller, of a 0.33 mean-width ratio. In this case, Formula 4-7 or Chart 4-2 gives a developed area of 304 square inches (1961 cm²). This produces a blade loading of 8.9 PSI (61360 N/m²), which is just 5 percent greater than the permissible loading from Formula 5-6. Although such a propeller might work acceptably, it would be safer to call for a 24-inch-diameter, four-bladed propeller of a 0.35 mean-width ratio. Its developed area of 322 square inches (2077 cm²) would lower blade loading to just under 8.5 PSI (58600 N/m²).

Supercavitating Propellers

For vessels operating at speeds over 35 knots, with shaft speeds in excess of 2,500 or 3,000 RPM, there is another option altogether—accept the cavitation. Propellers on such high-speed vessels are so highly loaded that cavitation actually becomes unavoidable. In these cases, the selection process would proceed as above for pitch and diameter, but you would choose a propeller model specifically designed to operate when fully cavitating. Since there is a wide variety of styles, make a final check with their manufacturers to determine the model best suited to your application.

Cupped-Bladed Propellers

An intermediate step for vessels operating at moderately high speeds (between 30 and 45 knots) is often possible. If the actual blade loading as determined from Formula 5-7 is only 10 to 15 percent over the allowable blade loading found from Formula 5-6, a propeller with cupped blades may be the answer. When specifying a cupped-bladed propeller, find pitch and diameter in the usual manner, and then decrease pitch by one inch or 5 percent, whichever is greater.

FINDING THRUST

Thrust at Speed

Thrust is the force, in pounds, generated by the propeller at a given speed. It is particularly important for workboats, which have to tow large loads and drive heavy hulls into rough seas. For pleasure craft, actually calculating thrust is less important, except that the more efficient the propeller, the more thrust it can deliver and the faster the boat will go at the same HP and RPM. Since we have worked through all the necessary calculations for *Svelte Samantha*, we will work through a sample thrust calculation using her as an example. (See also Chapter 8 regarding tugs and trawlers.) The thrust developed by a propeller may be found from Formula 5-8.

Formula 5-8   Thrust Formula

Formula 5-8

$$T = \frac{326 \times SHP \times e}{Va}$$

Where:
T = Thrust in pounds
SHP = Shaft horsepower at the propeller
e = Propeller efficiency
Va = Speed of water at the propeller, in knots (see "Wake Fraction," next chapter).

Thrust for *Svelte Samantha* at maximum RPM works out as follows: Shaft horsepower is 240 (179 kw), efficiency (from Chart 5-6) is 0.69, and Va is 19.76 knots:

$$T = \frac{326 \times 240\ SHP \times 0.69}{19.78\ Kts}$$

Therefore:
T = 2,729 pounds thrust

At a lower speed, say 12 knots (an SL ratio of 2.2), *Svelte Samantha*'s propeller would be absorbing about 106 HP (79 kw), according to Chart 2-1 or Formula 2-1. Water speed at the propeller would be a bit lower, say 93 percent or 11.1 knots (see section on wake fraction, Chapter 6). Slip will be higher, say around 34 percent (from Chart 5-2 or Formula 5-2). Accordingly, efficiency will be lower—around 0.63 (from Chart 5-6). Thus we would get:

$$T = \frac{326 \times 106\ SHP \times 0.63}{11.1\ Kts}$$

Therefore:
T = 1,961 pounds thrust (889 kgf)
These figures are approximations, since the precise figures for efficiency and slip are not known.

Static Thrust or Bollard Pull

With a boat running free, lower speed means lower thrust. When towing or tied to a dock, however, a vessel's low-speed thrust increases greatly because SHP goes up, while Va goes down. Thrust at maximum power with the boat tied to a dock is called *static thrust* or *bollard pull*. It cannot be properly estimated from Formula 5-8 because it calls for dividing by zero.

Determining static thrust is primarily of interest to tugboats. Barnaby gives a formula for estimating static thrust or bollard pull from SHP and propeller diameter:

Formula 5-9 Approximate Bollard Pull Formula

$T_s = 62.72 \times (SHP \times D/12)^{0.67}$

Where:

T_s = Static thrust or bollard pull, in pounds

SHP = Shaft horsepower at the propeller

D = Propeller diameter in inches

This formula may also be expressed as:

$T_s ton = 0.028 \times (SHP \times D_{ft})^{0.67}$

Where:

$T_s ton$ = Thrust in long tons of 2,240 pounds

SHP = Shaft horsepower

D_{ft} = Propeller diameter in feet

Formula 5-9

You can see that even at the same horsepower, the larger the propeller diameter, the greater the thrust. This reiterates the fact that for thrust at low to moderate speeds, large diameter is essential. Vessels intended for towing are equipped with large diameter propellers having wide blades and low shaft speeds—frequently under 500 RPM.

Planing vessels, designed for free running with high shaft speeds, will seldom generate more than 70 percent of the static thrust indicated by Formula 5-9, while some displacement vessels—not designed for towing, but with low shaft speeds and large propellers—may approach 85 or 90 percent of the static thrust indicated.

The rule of thumb for bollard pull is that a tug should develop about one ton of static thrust for every 100 BHP (75 kw) at the engine. This is a rough guide only, but it is handy for quick estimates and checking results.

VESSELS WITH MORE THAN ONE PROPELLER

Most Calculation Factors Remain the Same

The calculation for pitch is nearly the same for twin-screw vessels as for a single-screw craft, using Chart 5-1. After all, both propellers still have to advance the same distance as the boat each revolution. However, for lower speed craft (under 30 knots) slip will be slightly less, since the twin screws see a cleaner water flow without a skeg or deadwood ahead of them. The slip of 27 percent given on Chart 5-2 should be averaged against the value given in Table 5-3.

TABLE 5-3   TYPICAL SLIP VALUES—TWIN-SCREW VESSELS

Type of Boat	Speed in Knots	Percent of Slip
Auxiliary sailboats, barges	under 9	42%
Heavy powerboats, workboats	9–15	24%
Lightweight powerboats, cruisers	15–30	22%

TABLE 5-3

Above 30 knots, slip may be assumed to be the same for single- and twin-screw vessels. Use Table 5-1.

In the case of *Svelte Samantha,* the 27 percent slip from Chart 5-2 or Formula 5-2 (which was adjusted to 26 percent after comparison with Table 5-1) should be averaged with a slip of about 23 percent for a heavyish lightweight cruiser. This gives a slip of 25 percent. In this particular case, the pitch still works out to 26 inches (660 mm).

Diameter is found based on the SHP and RPM of each individual engine. If *Svelte Samantha* were powered by two engines delivering 120 BHP (89 kw) at 3,000 RPM, and each engine were fitted with a 2:1 reduction gear, shaft RPM would be 1,500. In this case, as we can see from Chart 5-3 or Formula 5-3, each engine could turn a 20-inch-diameter (508 mm) propeller. Chart 5-5 or Formula 5-5 indicate a minimum twin-screw diameter of 11.9 inches (302 mm), so a 20-inch (508 mm) propeller is more than adequate. The combined disc area of the twin screws (or triple screws) should be at least 25 percent more than the disc area of a single screw. When estimating slip on a triple-screw craft, the procedure for a single-screw vessel should be used on the centerline screw, while the method for estimating slip on twin-screw vessels should be used on outboard propellers.

Finally, we must check the individual propellers for cavitation using blade-loading Formulas 5-6, 5-7, Approximate Efficiency vs Slip Chart 5-6, and Developed Area Formula 4-6 or Chart 4-2: however, the SHP and RPM for each individual propeller is used in Formulas 5-6 and 5-7, while top speed under both engines combined is used to find the Va at the propellers. For the twin-screw *Svelte Samantha*, diameter = 20 in. (508 mm); pitch = 26 in. (660 mm); pitch ratio = 1.3; slip = 0.25; MWR = 0.33; developed area = 165 sq. in. (1064 cm²); efficiency = 0.72; and Va = 19.8 kts. Again, we find that blade loading with the 0.33 MWR propellers is 8.6 PSI (59290 N/m²)—just over what is permissible. Blades with 0.35 MWR reduce loading to acceptable levels.

DESIGNING FOR LIMITED DIAMETER

When Draft or Hull Shape Limits Diameter

Up to now, we have been calculating propellers as if there were little or no restriction on diameter. For *Svelte Samantha*, we have selected either a 26-inch-diameter by 26-inch-pitch (660 mm by 660 mm) three-bladed propeller, of 0.4 MWR, or a 24-inch-diameter by 25-inch-pitch (609 mm by 635 mm) four-bladed propeller, of 0.35 MWR. These propellers, however, are both a bit large for a vessel with only a 1 foot 4 inch (0.4 m) molded draft of hull. The total draft of such an installation could easily be 44 inches (1118 mm) or more. What if our single-screw installation is limited to 16 inches (406 mm) in diameter?

First we have to check Chart 5-5 or Formula 5-5 to see that this is not smaller than the minimum allowable diameter. In this case, the minimum diameter is 14.9 inches (378 mm), so there's no problem. If we were being forced to consider a propeller smaller than this, that's a clue that something is out of kilter with the basic boat design. The only alternative might have been to go to twin screws.

Now let's turn to DIA-HP-RPM Chart 5-3 or Formula 5-3 and determine the RPM required for this diameter. For *Svelte Samantha*, we find that her 240 SHP (179 kw) engine can turn a 16-inch (406 mm) propeller at 2,264 RPM. We must now choose our engine and reduction gear combination to give close to this RPM at the propeller. Estimated speed (V) at 90 percent of RPM (2,037 RPMs) remains 19.5 knots, and slip remains the same 26 percent as calculated earlier. With this information we can find pitch from Chart 5-1 or Formula 5-1, which indicates a 15.7-inch (398 mm) pitch. Accordingly, we will specify a 16-inch-diameter by 16-inch-pitch propeller (406 mm by 406 mm). (Again, the fact that it is a square wheel is incidental.) Checking against Optimum Pitch Ratio Chart 5-4 or Formula 5-4a, we find that a pitch ratio of 1 is excellent for this type of vessel.

Next, we'll check for cavitation, as before. Depth increases allowable blade loading only slightly, so we can use the same 8.5 PSI (58600 N/m²) we found earlier. The slip and pitch ratios have remained the same; efficiency (e) or (η) remains 0.69. For a MWR of 0.33, Formula 4-7 or Chart 4-2 give a developed blade area (A_d) of 101 square inches (652 cm²). Next, we find the actual blade loading from Formula 5-7:

$$PSI = \frac{326 \times 240 \text{ SHP} \times 0.69}{19.78 \text{ Kts} \times 101 \text{ sq. in.}}$$

Therefore:

$PSI = 27$ (186140 N/m²)—very high blade loading!

This is in the supercavitating region. But, of course, this makes sense, since we are trying to drive the same boat with a much smaller propeller. The same thrust is concentrated on a smaller area, raising blade loading tremendously. In fact, as we noted earlier, we still require the same 324 square inches (2090 cm²) of blade area to reduce blade loading to acceptable levels. Even a four-bladed propeller with a mean-width ratio of 0.55 would provide only 225 square inches (1452 cm²) of A_d. Since the 18 to 21 knots at which *Svelte Samantha* is intended to operate is too slow for a supercavitating propeller, we cannot drive her reliably with a propeller just 16 inches (406 mm) in diameter.

Determining Minimum Propeller Size From Blade Loading

How small a propeller could we use? Entering our minimum blade area of 324 square inches (2090 cm²) and maximum standard mean-width ratio of 0.55 into Formula 4-7 or Chart 4-2 gives a four-bladed propeller 19 inches (482 mm) in diameter. We can take this diameter and repeat the above process to find slip, pitch, and so on.

Drawbacks of a Propeller with Too Little Blade Area

What if you still want a bare 16 inches (406 mm) in diameter? This is a real problem. You'll have to accept a noticeable loss in efficiency. Either the propeller will cavitate at least some of the time, or a propeller with either very wide blades or more than four blades, or both, will be required. These alternatives will result in a loss of top speed and require operating the engine at higher RPMs to achieve cruising speed. The obvious alternative is to use twin screws. Interestingly, if *Svelte Samantha* were a somewhat higher speed craft—operating above 35 knots—we could forget about cavitation and go to a true supercavitating propeller.

Drawbacks of a Propeller of Smaller Diameter

Assuming we settle on the acceptable minimum 19-inch-diameter (482 mm) propeller, what have we lost by going with this smaller size? There are few disadvantages at cruising speed and above. At low speeds, however, this propeller will deliver less oomph—crash stops will take longer, and working into a tight slip by reversing to back to port will be less effective. The small propeller will not be as effective in powering into a head sea, and it will take a bit longer to force the boat up onto a plane. Once at speed, though, the difference in performance will be slight.

HIGH–SPEED PROPELLERS—OVER 35 KNOTS

Use Smaller Diameters at High Speed

Whereas larger-diameter propellers are better on low- and moderate-speed vessels, for speeds over 35 knots it is desirable to reduce propeller diameter. This is because the drag force of the water rushing past the hull increases as the square of boat speed, V. Accordingly, the resistance or appendage drag of a large propeller, its strut, and its shaft quickly become serious drawbacks.

If all-around handling and heavy-weather performance are desired along with high speed, it may still be worthwhile to use a large-diameter propeller and accept the somewhat reduced top speed caused by its drag. This is especially so for lower-end high-speed vessels, like sportfishermen and crew boats—vessels that operate in all weather and seldom exceed 40 or 45 knots. When all-out top speed is desired, however, and V exceeds 40 to 45 knots, propellers of the minimum diameter from Chart 5-5 or Formula 5-5 should be used.

Let's consider a flat-out, deep-vee ocean racer, *Rambling Rocket*. Her characteristics are:

Rambling Rocket		
40 ft.	12.2 m	LOA (length overall)
35 ft.	10.7 m	WL (waterline length)
10.5 ft.	3.2 m	BOA (beam overall)
9 ft.	2.7 m	BWL (waterline beam)
1.42 ft.	0.43 m	Hd (hull draft)
9,600 lb	4350 kg	Displacement

She is powered by twin engines delivering 450 BHP (335 kw) each at 4,400 RPM. We want to select the propellers that will give her maximum speed.

Determining RPM for Finding Diameter and Pitch

Rambling Rocket is not a sensible boat. Economy of operation and long engine life are not important. We simply want her to be able to blast along as fast as possible. Since she is laid out from the start for speed, we can assume that power losses from transmission, shafting, exhaust backpressure and auxiliary machinery are very low. Accordingly, we will select *Rambling Rocket*'s propellers based entirely on top engine RPM and SHP.

Entering *Rambling Rocket*'s waterline beam times her hull draft (a value of 12.78 sq. ft. or 82.5 cm²) in Chart 5-5 or Formula 5-5 yields a minimum diameter of 14.5 inches (368 mm). Since we are going all out for speed, let's round down and use a 14-inch (355 mm) diameter. Entering 14 inches and 450 SHP per engine in Chart 5-3, we find that shaft RPMs should be 4,393, which is so close to the top engine RPM of 4,400 as to make no difference. This gives us direct drive, meaning no reduction gear power losses, somewhat justifying our optimistic power loss estimates.

Planing Speed Chart 2-3 or Formula 2-4 predict a top speed of 64 knots (73 MPH) based on a total of 900 SHP (671 kw), or 10.6 LB/HP (6.4 kg per kw). Chart 5-2 or Formula 5-2 give a slip of 14.9 percent at that speed, while Table 5-1 suggests a 10 percent slip. We thus compromise on 12 percent. Pitch, from Chart 5-1 or Formula 5-1, is then 20.1 inches. Thus we specify two 14-inch-diameter by 20-inch-pitch propellers (355 mm by 508 mm), of a standard 0.33 mean-width ratio. This gives a pitch ratio of 1.43. From Optimum Pitch Ratio Chart 5-4 or Formula 5-4a, we can see that this is acceptable for a boat running at 64 knots.

Supercavitating Propellers at High Speed

Now we'll check for cavitation. Allowable pressure to cavitation, from Formula 5-6, is:

$$PSI = 1.9 \times 64 \text{ kts}^{0.5} \times 1.3 \text{ Ft}^{0.08}$$

Therefore:

$$PSI = 15.5 \ (106858 \text{ N/m}^2) \text{ before cavitation.}$$

Actual blade loading from Blade Loading Formula 5-7 is:

$$PSI = \frac{326 \times 450 \text{ SHP} \times 0.78}{64 \text{ Kts} \times 78 \text{ sq. in.}}$$

Therefore:

$$PSI = 22.9 \ (157900 \text{ N/m}^2) \text{ blade loading.}$$

With blade loading this high, the propellers will be cavitating all the time. Thus, we have to specify supercavitating propellers, which are about 90 percent as efficient as comparable noncavitating propellers. To avoid cavitation, we would have to specify a much larger propeller and much lower shaft speed, with substantially more area to lower the blade pressure. Unfortunately, at a speed of 64 knots, the additional appendage resistance from such a large propeller would far outweigh the relatively small gain in efficiency.

EVALUATING THE SLIP METHOD

The slip method of determining propellers has been tried and proved for well over half a century. It is widely used by many small craft designers and representatives of some propeller companies, and is acceptable for vessels where maximum efficiency is not critical, or for sailing auxiliaries, where performance under power is secondary. Carefully applying the slip method will result in selecting a satisfactory propeller. For best results, though, particularly in commercial applications, the Bp-δ method described in the next chapter is more accurate. In any case, the charts and tables of the slip method constitute an excellent means of making a preliminary propeller estimate, which may then be refined with the Bp-δ method.

Chapter 6
The Bp-δ Method
The Power Factor Method for Calculating Propellers

In the previous chapter we selected propellers by *estimating* apparent slip. In order to eliminate this estimate, we have to take a closer look at the relationship of the propeller's speed through the water, boat speed and theoretical propeller advance—pitch times RPM.

WAKE AND SPEED OF ADVANCE (Va)

Real and Apparent Slip

Figure 6-1 shows these relationships graphically. P × N represents the total distance the propeller would advance if there were no slip, as we discussed in Chapter 5. V represents boat speed. This is the speed of the boat through the water, as measured far enough away from the hull so that wake is not a factor. SlipA (apparent slip) is the difference between boat speed (V) and P × N. This is all exactly as shown in Figure 5-1.

As a boat moves forward, it drags along a fair amount of water. Water sticks to the hull (and the propeller) slightly because of friction before falling away astern, forming the *wake*. Because of this, the water the propeller actually "sees" is already moving forward a bit. In other words, the propeller is not advancing through the water as fast as boat speed (V). If, for instance, V were 10 knots and the hull were dragging along a wake of 1 knot, the propeller would be advancing through the water at only 9 knots.

Speed of Advance (Va)

W on Figure 6-1 represents this wake. If the wake (W) is added to the apparent slip we get the *real slip (SlipR)*. The difference between real slip (SlipR) and P × N (theoretical propeller advance) gives the actual speed of the propeller through the water it "sees"— speed of advance through the wake. This speed is almost universally known as *Va* or *speed of advance*.

Taylor Wake Fraction (Wt)

Admiral Taylor defined the wake as a percentage of boat speed (V); his formula is called the *Taylor wake fraction (Wt)*.

Formula 6-1   Taylor Wake Fraction Formula

Formula 6-1

$$Wt = \frac{V - Va}{V} \text{ or}$$

$$Va = V \times (1 - Wt)$$

Where:

Wt = Taylor wake fraction

V = Boat speed through water

Va = Speed of water at the propeller

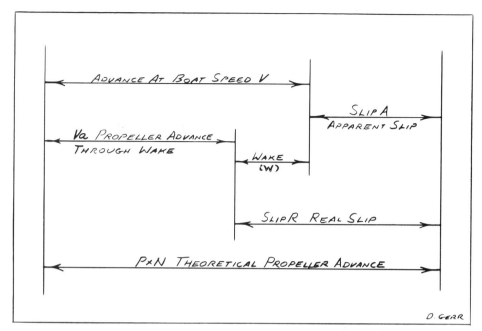

Figure 6-1

Slip, wake, and speed of advance.

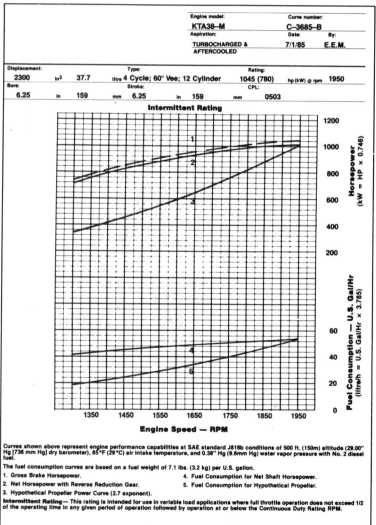

Figure 6-2

The engine performance curve of a Cummins KTA38-M.

(Courtesy of Cummins Engine Company, Inc.)

Wake Factor (Wf)

Obviously, in order to select a propeller as accurately as possible, we must allow for the wake and use Va, not V, in our work. It is convenient when using Formula 6-1 to give the value "1 − Wt" a name, and we will call it the *wake factor (Wf)*. (This should not be confused with Froude's wake fraction, which is also known as "Wf." Froude's wake fraction is seldom used, because it defines wake in terms of Va and not V. It is thus not as convenient for propeller calculations as the Taylor wake fraction, Wt.)

Formula 6-2   Wake Factor Formula

Formula 6-2

Wf = 1 − Wt

From this we can restate Formula 6-1 as:

Formula 6-3   Speed of Advance Formula

Formula 6-3

Va = V × Wf

Where:

V = Boat speed

Wf = Wake factor

Wt = Taylor wake fraction

Determining Wake Factor (Wf) From Block Coefficient— Displacement Vessels

Chart 6-1 plots wake factor (Wf) as a function of block coefficient (see Formula 6-5) for single- and twin-screw craft, and is applicable to vessels that operate with SL ratios of under 2.5. Vessels with higher block coefficients are fuller-bodied (tubbier). Accordingly, water flows around their hulls less easily and their wakes are greater than those with finer, more slender hulls. As you can see, the smallest wake factor, and thus the largest difference between V and Va, appears for craft with large block coefficients.

CHART 6-1   WAKE FACTOR VS BLOCK COEFFICIENT

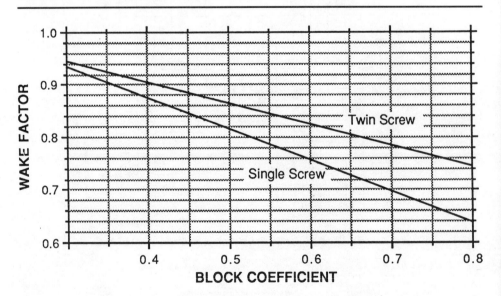

Chart 6-1.   *Wake factor as a function of block coefficient for single- and twin-screw craft with S-L ratios of less than 2.5. Based on Formula 6-5.*

Wake factors of single-screw craft are smaller (there is more wake) than for twin-screw vessels because the single propeller is partially hidden behind the keel, deadwood and/or skeg. By comparison, each propeller on a twin-screw craft "sees" a relatively unobstructed water flow (less wake).

The formulas below relating to the curves on Chart 6-1 were derived by the author and are based on data from Barnaby and from Caterpillar Inc.

Wake Factor vs Block Coefficient Formulas:

Formula 6-4a—Single Screw:

$$Wf = 1.11 - (0.6 \times Cb)$$

Formula 6-4b—Twin Screw:

$$Wf = 10.6 - (0.4 \times Cb)$$

Where:

Wf = Wake factor (percent of V "seen" by the propeller)

Cb = Block coefficient of hull

and

Formula 6-4a, b

Formula 6-5   Block Coefficient Formula

$$Cb = \frac{Disp}{WL \times BWL \times Hd \times 64 \text{ lb./cu.ft.}}$$

Disp = Displacement, in pounds

WL = Waterline length, in feet

BWL = Waterline beam, in feet

Hd = Hull draft, excluding keel, skeg or deadwood, in feet

Formula 6-5

The block coefficient may frequently be found on the lines drawing from the original designer. If it is not known, it may be calculated using Formula 6-5. Should the quantities for this formula be unknown, they can be found by measuring the hull as described in Appendix A.

Determining Wake Factor (Wf) from Speed—Planing Craft

Chart 6-2 plots wake fraction as a function of speed for twin-screw vessels that operate at planing speeds—those with SL ratios greater than 2.5. Values for single-screw vessels may be taken as 98 to 99 percent of those given in the chart. The final value for wake factor (Wf) may not exceed 99 percent. The curve is defined by a formula derived by the author, based on data from Du Cane, Lord and Phillips-Birt:

Formula 6-6   Wake Factor vs Speed Formula

$$Wf = 0.83 \times Kts^{0.047}$$

Where:

Wf = Wake Factor

Kts = Speed in knots

Formula 6-6

CHART 6-2   WAKE FRACTION VS SPEED

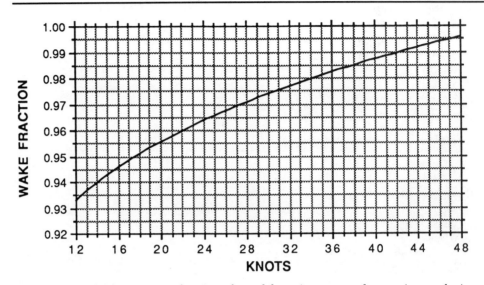

Chart 6-2.   *Wake fraction as a function of speed for twin-screw craft operating at planing speeds. Based on Formula 6-6.*

WORKING THROUGH A Bp-δ CALCULATION

Characteristics of Our Example Vessel—*Ocean Motion*

Now that we can determine Va, we can go ahead and begin to calculate a propeller using the Bp-δ method. Let us consider the propeller for the single-screw *Ocean Motion*. She might be a charter boat, a dive boat, a combination boat, or a large motor yacht. Keep in mind that the Bp-δ calculations and the other formulas given in this book will work for nearly every vessel, and *Ocean Motion* could have vastly differing specifications. Since we need specific numbers for our calculations, though, let's assume that her characteristics are as follows:

		Ocean Motion
100 ft.	30.48 m	LOA (length overall)
92 ft.	28.04 m	LWL (length waterline)
26 ft.	7.92 m	BOA (beam overall)
25 ft.	7.62 m	BWL (beam waterline)
9.75 ft.	2.96 m	Hd (hull draft)
10.5 ft.	3.20 m	Maximum draft
225.8 tons	229.4 Mtons	Displacement (long tons and metric tons)
505,830 lb	229440 kg	Displacement
290	290	DL ratio (displacement/length ratio)
74 in.	188 cm	Maximum propeller diameter to fit within existing aperture
4.2 ft.	1.28 m	Shaft centerline below waterline

Her operator wishes to run at a continuous speed of 12.2 knots (which works out to a speed/length ratio of 1.27), with a bit extra in reserve. This is a practical operating speed for a displacement vessel of this size, although reducing continuous operating speed to 11.5 knots would save around 20 percent in power and fuel requirements (see Chapter 2). From Chart 2-1 or Formula 2-1, we determine that *Ocean Motion* requires one horsepower at the shaft per 575 pounds of displacement (one kw per 350 kg) to make this speed. At her displacement of 505,830 pounds (229440 kg), this comes to 880 SHP (656 kw).

A vessel of this size should be equipped with a true marine diesel. An intermittent rating would be appropriate for the intended use—a continuous cruising speed with some extra power in reserve. Accordingly, we would plan on operating at about 85 percent of top RPM and HP (see Chapter 1). We also have to allow for a 3 percent loss of power due to bearing friction and exhaust back pressure. This indicates an engine with a maximum BHP rating of 1,066 HP (795 kw) **[880 SHP ÷ 0.85 = 1,009 HP, and 1,009 HP × 1.03 = 1066 BHP]**. At this point, we must consult various manufacturers to determine which engines meet these requirements. One such engine would be a Cummins KTA38-M. In the intermittent rating it delivers a top power of 1,045 HP (780 kw) at 1,950 RPM, and it puts out 990 HP (738 kw) at its maximum safe continuous operating speed of 1,800 RPM. We are planning to operate continuously at 85 percent of top RPM or 1,657 RPM at 882 HP (658 kw). Figure 6-3 shows the performance curves for this engine.

Estimating Shaft Speed (RPM or N)

We must now make a starting estimate of a suitable shaft speed to determine the proper reduction gear ratio. This may be done by referring to Minimum Diameter Chart 5-5 or Formula 5-5 and then referring to the DIA-HP-RPM Formula 5-3. The minimum diam-

CHART 6-3   ENLARGED SECTION OF A Bp = δ CHART

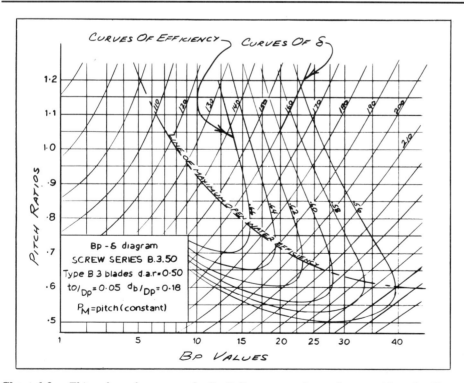

Chart 6-3. *This enlarged segment of a Bp-δ diagram can be used as a guide to familiarize yourself with the full Bp-δ diagrams in Chart 6-4.*

eter indicated is 64 inches. Next, enter the largest-diameter propeller that will fit in the available propeller aperture (74 inches) and the maximum shaft horsepower our engine can deliver into Formula 5-3. From this we find the RPM. Maximum SHP is about 1,020 (760 kw) (assuming that with everything wide open the propeller will see about 97 percent of maximum brake HP).

Thus, if *Ocean Motion* has room for a 74-inch-diameter (188 cm) propeller, her maximum shaft speed would be about 360 RPM. Top engine RPM is 1,950, so the reduction ratio should be 5.4:1 (1,950 RPM ÷ 360 RPM = 5.4). (In practice, you may not be able to find a gear of the exact reduction ratio calculated. In this case, you have to settle for the nearest commercially available gear ratio. You must also consider whether a vee drive, angled drive or offset drive is required, and how this can either be incorporated into the reverse/reduction gear or mated with it.)

Checking Shaft Speed Against Other Similar Vessels

It is now a good idea to check this shaft speed against that of comparable vessels to see if both the available propeller aperture and the engine chosen are suitable. Although we'll make the final determination of suitable shaft speed from the Bp-δ diagrams, it makes matters simpler to start with a good estimate. Table 6-1 gives typical shaft speeds for various types of vessels and various speed-length ratios.

TABLE 6-1   SUGGESTED SHAFT SPEEDS

TABLE 6-1

Type of Vessel	SL Ratio	Range of Shaft RPM
Heavy displacement hulls (tugs, push boats, heavy fishing vessels)	under 1.2	250–500
Medium-to-light displacement hulls (fishing vessels, trawlers, workboats, trawler yachts)	under 1.45	300–1,000
Semidisplacement hulls (Crew boats, patrol boats, motoryachts)	1.45–3.0	800–1,800
Planing hulls (yachts, fast commuters and ferries, high-speed patrol boats)	over 3.0	1,200–3,000 +

Inspection of Table 6-1 indicates that a shaft speed of 360 RPMs is suitable for a vessel like *Ocean Motion*. (Shaft speeds at the lower end of the recommended range indicate larger propeller diameters, which is good.) If the shaft RPM we derived from Chart 5-3 or Formula 5-3, based on the capacity of the propeller aperture, is significantly higher than the speed recommended in Table 6-1, the available propeller aperture is too small for the hull. A propeller can be found that will work, but it will never be as efficient as a larger-diameter propeller with the lower shaft speed recommended in Table 6-1.

Similarly, if the largest diameter that will fit in the propeller aperture is smaller than indicated on Minimum Diameter Chart 5-5, the aperture is too small for the hull. Again, a propeller can be selected that will work, but at lower efficiencies than one of larger diameter.

The Bp-δ Diagrams or Charts

We now have sufficient information to enter the Bp-δ charts and determine the most suitable propeller. Charts 6-4A, B, C, and D have been prepared based on open-water tests run by Admiral David Taylor and later by Troost and others. After data from open-water tests have been collected, they are entered on the Bp-δ chart for propellers of each pattern. The dense format of these charts may be intimidating at first to readers with nontechnical backgrounds, but you should not let this deter you from using them. Once you have run through a calculation with the Bp-δ diagrams, you will find them very clear and accessible.

The type of propeller covered by a given Bp-δ diagram is described in the legend in the corner. For instance "Screw Series B.3.50" is for three-bladed, type B (average type) ogival-section propellers, with a disc area ratio of 0.50 and constant face pitch. As we have seen from Formula 4-4, this corresponds to blades with a mean-width ratio of 0.33 for propellers with the average 20-percent hub diameter.

Power Factor (Bp) and Advance Coefficient (δ)

To use these charts, we must be able to calculate the value of Bp, which is known as the *power coefficient* or *power factor* (occasionally the *basic variable*) and the value of δ (delta), which is known as the *speed coefficient* or *advance coefficient*.

Formula 6-7 *Power Factor Formula*

$$Bp = \frac{(SHP)^{0.5} \times N}{Va^{2.5}}$$

Where:

Bp = Power factor

SHP = Shaft horsepower at the propeller

N = Shaft RPM

Va = Speed of advance of the propeller through the wake

Formula 6-7

Formula 6-8 *Advance Coefficient Formula*

$$\delta = \frac{N \times Dft}{Va} \text{ or } \frac{N \times D}{12 \times Va}$$

This may also be restated as:

$$D = \frac{\delta \times Va \times 12}{N}$$

Where:

δ = Advance coefficient

N = Shaft RPM

Dft = Propeller diameter in feet

D = Propeller diameter in inches

Va = Speed of advance of the propeller through the wake

Formula 6-8

Determining Va

In using the Bp-δ charts, we always use maximum SHP and RPM—not maximum brake horsepower, but maximum horsepower delivered to the propeller. First, we find Va. For *Ocean Motion,* this works out as follows:

Using Formula 6-5 to determine the block coefficient,

$$Cb = \frac{505,830 \text{ lb. Disp.}}{92 \text{ ft. WL} \times 25 \text{ ft. BWL} \times 9.75 \text{ ft. Hd} \times 64 \text{ lb./cu.ft}}$$

Therefore:

Cb = 0.35

From Chart 6-1 or Formula 6-4, we find that the Wf (wake factor) for a vessel with a block coefficient of 0.35 is 0.9. *Ocean Motion*'s top speed, at maximum RPM, will be based on top SHP (not BHP) of 1,020 HP (760 kw)—about 97 percent of top BHP. This yields one horsepower per 496 pounds (one kw per 302 kg). Chart 2-1 or Formula 2-1 give an SL ratio of 1.34, for a boat speed (V) of 12.8 knots. Va is thus 11.5 knots [**12.8 knot V × 0.9 Wf = 11.5 knot Va**].

Calculating Bp—The Power Factor

Next, we determine Bp using Formula 6-7:

$$Bp = \frac{(1{,}020 \ SHP)^{0.5} \times 360 \ RPM}{11.5 \ knts^{2.5}}$$

Therefore:

Bp = 25.6

Determining δ—The Advance Coefficient

We can now enter the Bp-δ diagram for the propeller pattern of our choice, with the Bp value. We run up from the Bp value till we cross the dot-dash line of maximum open-water efficiency (see the enlargement of a Bp-δ diagram, Chart 6-3). The value for δ is now interpolated from the δ-curve that crosses the line of maximum open-water efficiency at the point closest to its intersection with Bp = 25.6 (or just above). On this chart, the δ value is 215.

The δ value determines diameter, but the Bp-δ charts reflect the results of open water tests without a hull ahead of the propeller. Accordingly, we have to adjust the δ value to reflect the presence of a hull ahead of the propeller by multiplying the following percentages:

TABLE 6-2   δ VALUE ADJUSTMENTS

TABLE 6-2

Number of Propellers	% Adjustment
Single screw	0.95
Twin screw	0.97

For a triple-screw vessel, use the single-screw value for the centerline propeller and the twin-screw value for the wing propellers. Adjusting δ in this way increases pitch to make proper allowance for the effect of wake, and reduces efficiency, to reflect the reduced efficiency of the propeller being behind the hull.

Calculating Diameter (D) from Advance Coefficient (δ)

For the single-screw *Ocean Motion,* we thus multiply the δ of 215 by 0.95, from Table 6-2, to get an adjusted δ of 204.2 We can now solve for diameter using Formula 6-8:

$$D = \frac{204.2 \times 11.5 \ kts \times 12}{360 \ RPM}$$

Therefore:

D = 78.3 inches

Adjusting δ to Obtain a Smaller Diameter (D)

We have already determined that the maximum diameter that can be accommodated in *Ocean Motion*'s propeller aperture is 74 inches. We thus have several options. We can (1) choose a lower value of δ, which will cross the Bp = 25.6 line above the line of optimum efficiency; (2) return to the beginning of our Bp-δ calculation and try a higher shaft speed to reduce diameter; or (3) try a different propeller pattern on another Bp-δ diagram. To determine the δ value that will give us a 74-inch (188 cm) propeller of three blades with a DAR of 0.5 at our present RPM, we'll use Formula 6-8 times the adjustment factor from Table 6–2. Inserting the maximum allowable diameter, we get:

$$\delta = \frac{360 \text{ RPM} \times 74 \text{ in. Dia}}{12 \times 11.5 \text{ kts}} \times 0.95 \text{ adjustment factor}$$

Therefore:

δ = 183.4 for a 74-inch (188 cm) propeller

Finding Efficiency (e) or (η)

The δ = 183.4 curve intersects the Bp = 25.6 line just about where the efficiency (η) curve is 0.58. In other words, the efficiency of a propeller with this diameter, Bp, and δ would be 58 percent. This is an acceptable efficiency, so we can continue and determine pitch.

Determining Pitch (P)

At this point we have settled on a 74-inch (188 cm) diameter three-bladed propeller with a DAR of 0.5, a power factor (Bp) of 25.6, and an advance coefficient (δ) of 183.4. Running from the intersection of δ = 183.4 and Bp = 25.6 horizontally across to the left side of the Bp-δ diagram, we find the pitch ratio. (The Bp-δ charts label pitch ratio as ^{P}M/Dp, which simply means "pitch mean" divided by "diameter propeller.") In case of *Ocean Motion,* we find a pitch ratio of 0.94. Simply multiplying the diameter by the pitch ratio gives pitch, so pitch is 69.5 inches (176 cm) **[0.94 pitch ratio × 74 in. dia. = 69.5 inches]**. Where stock propellers over 36 inches in diameter are available in 2-inch increments of diameter, and 1-inch increments of pitch, we would call for a 74-inch (188 cm) diameter by 70-inch (178 cm) pitch propeller.

Finding Thrust

If the thrust of the propeller is required, Formulas 5-8 and 5-9 should be used as described in Chapter 5; however, efficiency (e) or (η) should now be taken directly from the Bp-δ diagrams, rather than from Chart 5-6.

Checking for Cavitation

Finally, we must check for cavitation using the blade-loading method as described in Chapter 5. From chart 4-2 or Formula 4-6, we determine that the developed area of a 74-inch-diameter, three-bladed propeller of 0.5 DAR (thus about 0.33 MWR) is 2,149 square inches (13865 cm²). *Ocean Motion*'s top speed (Va) at 1,020 SHP (760 kw) is 11.5 knots. Her shaft centerline is 4.2 feet (1.28 m) below the waterline at the propeller, and the propeller efficiency (η) we have determined as 0.58. Inserting this information into Formula 5-6 yields the maximum blade loading before cavitation as 7.2 PSI (49637 N/m²). The actual blade loading, from Formula 5-7 is 8.0 PSI (55497 N/m²). Accordingly, this propeller may experience cavitation. Thus, we proceed to increase the total area of the propeller, as in Chapter 5, by increasing blade width (MWR and DAR), or increasing the number of blades, or both. With the Bp-δ charts, however, we reenter the diagram for the new propeller pattern with our Bp value and repeat the calculations to find the appropriate δ, efficiency, pitch ratio and pitch.

In the case of *Ocean Motion,* Formulas 4-6 and 5-7 show that a propeller with a MWR of 0.37 would reduce blade loading to just under 7.2 PSI (49637 N/m²). The loss in efficiency from this small increase in blade width is negligible. In fact, we may enter our Bp value of 25.6 and our adjusted δ of 183.4 on the Bp-δ diagram for 3-bladed propellers of 0.65 DAR (about 0.42 MWR). We would find a new efficiency (η) of 0.56 and a pitch ratio of 0.95. These give the same pitch, 70 inches (178 cm), and the same predicted speed as the 0.33 MWR/0.50 DAR propeller we started with. The wider blades, however, ensure that cavitation will not be a problem.

Calculations for Twin-Screw Craft

If *Ocean Motion* had been a twin-screw vessel, we would have calculated the individual propellers exactly as with the single screw above. The horsepower and shaft speed, of course, would have been based on the SHP and RPM delivered to each individual propeller, while boat speed (V) and speed of advance (Va) would have been based on the total SHP of the two engines and propellers combined.

APPLYING THE Bp-δ DIAGRAMS TO PROPELLERS OF DIFFERENT PATTERNS

Propellers of Differing DAR or MWR

The four Bp-δ diagrams (Charts 6-4A, B, C, and D) at the end of this chapter cover three-bladed propellers of 0.50 and 0.65 disc area ratios, and four-bladed propellers of 0.40 and 0.55 disc area ratios. The blade patterns are elliptical, with no skew, fully ogival or flat-faced section, constant face pitch, a blade thickness fraction of 0.05, and a hub or boss 18 percent of diameter. This covers the majority of stock propellers. For propellers of slightly greater or lesser DAR ratios, using the chart with the closest DAR will give adequate accuracy.

Efficiency Adjustment Table 6-3 gives the change in efficiency for propellers of the same diameter but with differing disc-area ratios and mean-width ratios.

TABLE 6-3 EFFICIENCY ADJUSTMENT TABLE
Disc Area Ratios (DAR)

Pitch Ratio	0.30	0.50	0.65	0.80	0.90
1.4	1.010	1.000	0.970	0.950	0.920
1.2	1.150	1.000	0.965	0.930	0.900
1.0	1.020	1.000	0.960	0.920	0.880
0.8	1.025	1.000	0.950	0.900	0.960
0.6	1.030	1.000	0.940	0.880	0.840

TABLE 6-3

All the above factors are related to a standard propeller with a DAR of 0.50, which is taken as unity (1.000) on the table. To find the efficiency of a propeller with a differing DAR, multiply by the appropriate factor from Table 6-3. For example, if we know that a four-bladed propeller of 0.50 DAR had a pitch ratio of 1.2 and an efficiency (η) of 0.55, and wish to find the efficiency (η) of a four-bladed propeller of 0.90 DAR and a 1.2 pitch ratio, we multiply 0.55 by 0.90 to find that the wider-bladed propeller has an η of 0.49.

The ratios may be interpolated for propellers with DARs falling between the values given on the table. In addition, if the efficiency (η) of a propeller of a DAR other than 0.5 is known, the η of a propeller of a differing DAR may be found from the ratio of the efficiencies presented. For example, if a three-bladed propeller with a pitch ratio of 1.0 and a DAR of 0.80 is known to have an η of 0.62, the efficiency of a similar propeller with a DAR of 0.90 would be 97 percent of the original propeller (From Table 6-3, **0.92 ÷ 0.95 = 0.968**) for an η of 0.60.

It is clear that moderate changes in blade width (MWR and DAR) make relatively small changes in efficiency.

Two-Bladed Propellers

For two-bladed propellers, calculate in the usual way, using the three-bladed Bp-δ diagram whose DAR ratio gives a MWR ratio as close as possible to the MWR of the blades on the two-bladed propeller. Then adjust the final results of the three-bladed propeller for a two-bladed propeller by multiplying by the factors given in Table 5-2. Remember to use the reduced developed area (Ad), of the two-bladed propeller in determining blade loading.

Propellers With Skew and/or Rake

Propellers with small to moderate amounts of skew or rake will have nearly the same values as non-skewed or non-raked propellers of the same diameter, pattern, and pitch ratio, and may be calculated from the standard Bp-δ diagram of the appropriate DAR and number of blades. The skewed or raked propeller will have slightly less efficiency than a non-skewed or non-raked standard propeller. (See Chapter 4 for the advantages and disadvantages of skew and rake.)

Propellers with Airfoil Section at Their Blade Roots

Propellers with airfoil section introduced at their roots and then returning to fully ogival section about halfway out along the blades can also be calculated using the standard series Bp-δ charts. Such propellers will actually have 2 to 4 percent greater efficiency than shown on these charts, but they will have an increased tendency to cavitate. Thus, this type of propeller should be avoided in situations where there is high blade loading. (See discussions in Chapter 4 on blade section shape.)

Supercavitating Propellers

The patterns of supercavitating propellers differ widely and, of course, they also differ from those of the standard Taylor-Troost series propellers. Accordingly, the standard Bp-δ charts are less accurate for supercavitating propellers than for other types of propellers. Nevertheless, in the absence of Bp-δ diagrams prepared for the specific pattern of supercavitating propeller being considered, the standard Bp-δ diagrams can be used. Select from the chart whose DAR and number of blades is closest to the supercavitating propeller in question. The supercavitating propeller will deliver roughly 90 percent of the efficiency of the standard-series, non-cavitating propeller.

PROPELLER EFFICIENCY AND PERFORMANCE

Efficiency Assumptions of Speed Estimate Formulas

Until now, we have discussed efficiency but we have not examined how it affects performance. Formula 5-8 shows that thrust increases directly with increased efficiency. Thus, the higher the efficiency (e) or (η), the faster a vessel will go with the same horsepower. Efficiency vs Slip Chart 5-6 is not accurate enough to use for determining the effect of efficiency on performance; however, the efficiency values from the Bp-δ charts are.

Our speed estimates are based on Displacement Speed Chart 2-1 or Formula 2-1, and Planing Speed Chart 2-3 or Formula 2-4. Both formulas assume a propeller has been selected that will deliver an efficiency of between 0.50 and 0.60, with 55 percent being a good average. If the propeller selected falls within these ranges of efficiency, we can assume that the speed estimates from these formulas will be accurate.

Estimating Displacement Speed with Propeller Efficiency (η)

When efficiencies fall outside these values, the speed estimate should be adjusted accordingly. For displacement hulls, the speed should be adjusted as the cube root of the ratio of actual propeller efficiency (η) to the assumed propeller efficiency of 0.55. Using this information we can rewrite Formula 2-1 to include propeller efficiency as follows:

Formula 6-9 Displacement Speed with Efficiency Formula

$$\text{SL RATIO} = \frac{10.665}{\sqrt[3]{\text{LB/SHP}}} \times \sqrt[3]{\frac{\eta}{0.55}}$$

Formula 6-9

Where:

SL RATIO = Speed-length ratio

LB = Displacement in pounds

SHP = Shaft horsepower at the propeller

η = Propeller efficiency

If speed in knots is already known, we can multiply the speed directly by

$$\sqrt[3]{\frac{\eta}{0.55}}$$

For *Ocean Motion,* we have selected a propeller that has an efficiency of 0.58. The cube root of $\eta = 0.58$ divided by assumed efficiency 0.55 is only 1.018. Thus, our earlier top speed estimate of 12.8 knots for *Ocean Motion* could be multiplied by 1.018, giving a new top speed of 13 knots. In practice, our speed estimates are only accurate to within about one-third to one-half of a knot. The improvement we are finding is below the threshold of accuracy for our estimating method, so we cannot count on getting this extra speed. We do know, however, that any propeller with a higher efficiency will give a superior performance to one with a lower efficiency.

If, however, the efficiency of the propeller we have chosen falls below the assumed efficiency range, then we should make allowances for it. If we had been forced, on *Ocean Motion,* to select a smaller-diameter propeller with a higher RPM, we might have been compelled to use a propeller that delivered an efficiency of only 0.48. In that case, *Ocean Motion*'s top speed would have fallen to 12.2 knots **[0.48 ÷ 0.55 = 0.87, and $\sqrt[3]{0.87}$ = 0.95, then 12.8 kts × 0.95 = 12.2 kts].** We would then take this new top speed (V) and recalculate Va, and then Bp and δ based on the new Va, to find the most suitable propeller.

Estimating Planing Speed with Propeller Efficiency (η)

Propellers for planing vessels that fall outside the assumed range of efficiency (0.50 to 0.60), as determined by Planing Speed Formula 2-4, should also be adjusted. For planing vessels, the speed estimate will vary as the square root of the ratio of propeller efficiency to assumed efficiency 0.55. Thus, we can rewrite Formula 2-4 to include propeller efficiency (η) as follows:

Formula 6-10 Planing Speed with Efficiency Formula

$$\text{Kts} = \frac{C}{\sqrt{\frac{\text{LB}}{\text{SHP}}}} \times \sqrt{\frac{\eta}{0.55}}$$

Formula 6-10

Where:

Kts = Boat speed in knots

LB = Displacement in pounds

SHP = Shaft horsepower at the propeller

η = Propeller efficiency

If speed in knots is already known, we can multiply the speed directly by:

$$\sqrt{\frac{\eta}{0.55}}$$

Keep in mind—before undertaking exacting recalculations—that our planing speed estimates are only accurate to within 2 to 4 knots. Accordingly, just as with Formula 6-9, there is little point in recalculating speed if η falls within the assumed range. When efficiency falls above or below the assumed range, however, the speed should be recalculated, and the new Va used to find new Bp and δ values.

The Importance of Using Large Diameter and Low RPM

Inspection of the Bp-δ diagrams shows that the highest propeller efficiencies are associated with low values of Bp and low values of δ. (A Bp of 4 and a δ of 80 would give an efficiency of 79 percent.) In other words, at low to moderate speeds (V and Va), for a given horsepower, the slower the shaft RPM and the larger the diameter the more efficient the propeller will be. This is true for every installation, unless boat speed will consistently be above 30 or 35 knots. Accordingly, in selecting a propeller you should always start with the largest diameter possible for the given hull, and work from there.

As V and Va get higher—approaching 35 knots and more—Bp values also drop, because the value of $Va^{2.5}$ grows very large, as do corresponding δ values. This naturally leads to the selection of smaller-diameter, high-pitch-ratio propellers. (See Chapter 5.)

Draft limitations, hull shape, and tip clearances (see Chapter 7) are nearly the only factors that should cause you to consider a smaller diameter for slow-to-moderate speed craft. Another practical limitation is that while reduction gears with ratios as great as 6 or 7 to 1 are available for larger marine engines of, say over 250 HP (185 kw), standard reduction gears—for smaller, high-speed automotive-conversion type engines—are seldom available with ratios larger than 3 to 1. If such an engine has a top speed of 3,800 RPM, a 3:1 reduction will only reduce shaft speed to 1,267 RPM, which may be higher than ideal for some vessels.

Unfortunately, there are many craft in service designed and fitted with propellers of smaller diameter than recommended by Minimum Diameter Chart 5-5 or Formula 5-5. If the existing hull, propeller-aperture, or shaft-strut configuration does not permit a larger propeller, you will have to use the largest workable diameter and settle for the lower efficiency and lower speed of such an installation. Alternatively, you can use this smaller diameter and substitute a more powerful engine to obtain the desired speed with this lower efficiency propeller. Formulas 6-9 and 6-10 will enable you to calculate how much additional horsepower will be required.

CONSIDERATIONS IN APPLYING THE Bp-δ METHOD

Slip and the Bp-δ Method

Throughout our discussion of the Bp-δ method, we have not referred to slip even once. The fact is that knowing slip serves no useful purpose here. The advance coefficient (δ) evaluates the relationship of theoretical propeller advance (P × N) and real propeller speed through the water (Va). Nevertheless, if you wish to determine slip, it is a simple matter to multiply P × N and divide it by boat speed V (not Va) to find apparent slip (SlipA). For *Ocean Motion,* with a top boat speed of 12.8 knots, a top shaft RPM of 360, and a propeller pitch of 70 inches (178 cm), we use Formula 5-1 to find that apparent slip (SlipA) is 0.38.

$$\text{SlipA} = \frac{[(70 \text{ in.}/12) \times 360 \text{ RPM}] - (12.8 \text{ kts} \times 101.3)}{(70 \text{ in.}/12) \times 360 \text{ RPM}}$$

Therefore:
SlipA = 0.38

CHART 6-4 Bp = δ CHARTS

Bp - δ diagram
SCREW SERIES B.4-55
Type B 4 blades d.a.r.=0.55
to/Dp=0.05 db/Dp=0.18
P_M=pitch at blade tip
Pitch reduction at
blade root = 20%

$$Bp = \frac{N P_D^{0.5}}{Va^{2.5}} \qquad \delta = \frac{N Dp}{Va}$$

N = revs./min.
P_D = shp (1hp=76 kgm/sec.)
Dp = diameter in feet
Va = V_S (1-Wt) in Kn

$$Bp = \frac{N P_D^{0.5}}{Va^{2.5}} \qquad \delta = \frac{N Dp}{Va}$$

N = revs./min.
P_D = shp (1hp=76 kgm/sec.)
Dp = diameter in feet
Va = V_S (1-Wt) in Kn

Bp - δ diagram
SCREW SERIES B.3-65
Type B 3 blades d.a.r.=0.65
to/Dp=0.05 db/Dp=0.18
P_M=pitch (constant)

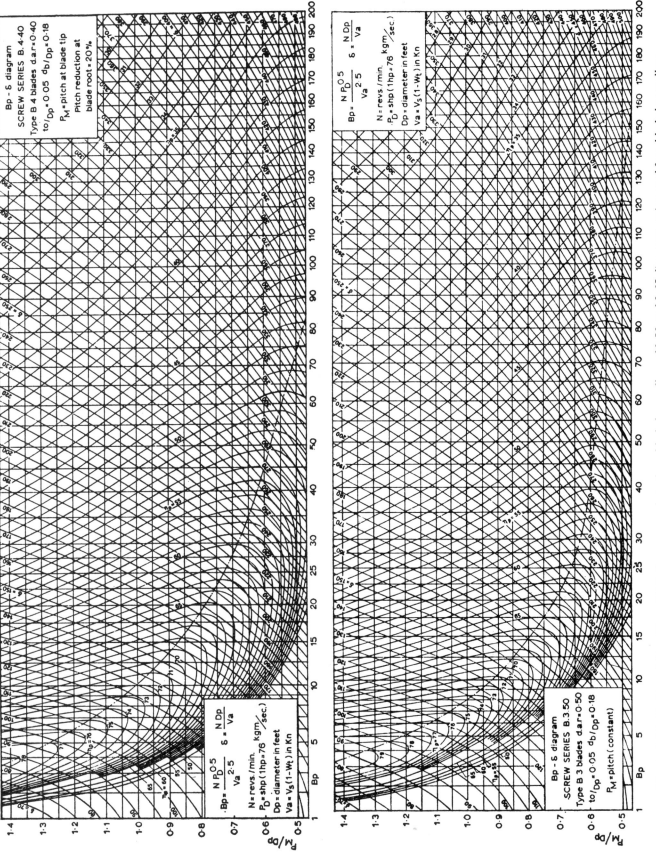

Charts 6-4 A, B, C, and D. These BP-δ diagrams apply to three-bladed propellers of 0.50 and 0.65 disc-area ratios, and four-bladed propellers of 0.40 and 0.55 disc-area ratios. The assumed blade patterns are elliptical, with no skew, a fully ogival or flat-faced section, a constant face pitch, a blade-thickness fraction of 0.05, and a hub or boss 18 percent of diameter, which covers the majority of stock propellers.

We can enter Approximate Efficiency vs Slip Chart 5-6 with a SlipA of 0.38 and *Ocean Motion*'s propeller pitch ratio of 0.94 to find that also gives an efficiency of around 0.58. But, we already knew this exactly from the Bp-δ chart. What's more, the Slip vs Boat Speed Chart 5-1 and Table of Typical Slips 5-1 would have given us a slip value of around 0.33 for *Ocean Motion*. This is the drawback to estimating slip. Such a slip value would have led us to specify a propeller with too little pitch. Once you have learned the Bp-δ method, you are better off without using slip.

Very High-Speed Craft and the Bp-δ Method

For light, very high-speed craft—vessels that operate over 50 or 60 knots—the Bp-δ method is not as useful. This is due to the very high values of $Va^{2.5}$, which make for very small Bp values. Let's look at the high-speed *Rambling Rocket* (our example from the last chapter), which is near the upper range of speed and HP that can be accommodated on the Bp-δ charts.

With twin 450-BHP (335 kw) engines, and SHP taken at maximum BHP, shaft RPM of 4,500, V of 64 knots, Va of 63.4 knots, and a 14-inch (355 mm)-diameter propeller, *Rambling Rocket*'s Bp is found to be 2.9, δ is 0.88, and 0.95δ is 0.83. The B.3.50 Bp-δ chart gives a pitch ratio of 1.38, for a 14-inch-diameter by 19-inch-pitch (355 mm by 483 mm) propeller—very close to the 14-inch by 20-inch propeller (355 mm by 508 mm) found using the slip method.

You can see, however, that if Bp had been much higher the intersections of δ and η would be off the upper left-hand corner of our Bp-δ diagram. Thus, for such very high-speed craft, we have to fall back on the slip method. This is not as bad as it seems because slip on such craft is very small (usually under 11 percent), as is the wake. Accordingly, there is less room for error in guesstimating slip than there is with moderate- and low-speed craft, for which wake and slip can vary tremendously.

Advantages of Bp-δ Method

Not only is the Bp-δ method more accurate than the slip method for most vessels, but it enables you very quickly and easily to try many different variables. If we had had to use a smaller diameter propeller on *Ocean Motion*—at the same RPM—we could quickly have solved for whatever value of δ would be suitable, using Formula 6-8 and Table 6-2. We could then immediately read off the new efficiency, pitch ratio and pitch. We could also quickly recalculate Bp for both higher RPM and smaller diameter, deriving suitable values for that combination. Just as easily, we could enter any of our Bp values on the charts for another propeller pattern (with wider blades, or more blades) to see how it would work out.

In fact, for designs in which the variables of shaft speed and propeller diameter are still wide open, a whole series of possible propellers of differing RPMs, diameters and patterns can be calculated. All critical values for each variation—Bp, δ, η, Wf, Va, V, Diameter, Pitch Ratio, Pitch, MWR, DAR, Ad, blade loading, thrust at important operating speeds, and so on—can then be listed in tabular form and easily compared. Critical values for each propeller may also be plotted against RPM. With this wealth of information, it becomes a relatively easy job to select the propeller that offers the best compromise of assets for a specific vessel and application.

Chapter 7
Installation Considerations
Blade Clearances, Shafting, and Propeller Weight

PROPELLER CLEARANCES

Tip Clearance

In the past few chapters, we have discussed the importance of using the largest-diameter propeller possible. For single-screw vessels, diameter is limited by the size or height of the propeller aperture. On twin-screw craft, the diameter is limited by the shortest distance from the centerline of the shaft-strut bearing up to the underside of the hull. For a new design, this distance can be found by measuring from the buttock lines at the half-breadth of the propeller shaft, and cross-checking on the sections or body plan at the location of the strut and propeller. On an existing vessel, the distance can be measured directly. (Remember that the shortest distance may not be straight up. When measuring, swing your ruler through an arc centered at the shaft centerline. The shortest distance will often be found with the ruler angled slightly up and inboard.)

Once you know the maximum distance from the shaft centerline to the hull (and down to the skeg below, in an aperture), you can determine the largest acceptable propeller diameter. Generally, there should be a *tip clearance* of at least 15 percent of the overall propeller diameter between the blade tips and the hull. The ideal tip clearance is 20 percent or more; however, additional tip clearance is usually found at the cost of overall propeller diameter. Since smaller diameters mean lower efficiency, you are faced with a trade-off between the increase in efficiency from larger diameter and the increase in efficiency from improved water flow to the propeller and reduced vibration from greater tip clearance.

Actually, the slower the shaft RPM and the lower the boat speed, the lower the minimum tip clearance may be. Minimum Tip Clearance Table 7-1 below gives minimum tip clearances at varying RPM.

TABLE 7-1   MINIMUM TIP CLEARANCE

RPM	SL Ratio	Minimum Tip Clearance
200–500	under 1.2	8%
300–1,800	1.2–2.5	10%
1,000 and above	over 2.5	15%
high-speed planing craft	over 3.0	20%

TABLE 7-1

The clearances in Table 7-1 represent the absolute minimum, so you should always strive to do better. Tugs and trawlers frequently accept the additional vibration of propellers with only 8 to 10 percent tip clearance to gain additional thrust at low speed from increased propeller diameter. On propellers in an aperture or with a protective skeg below, the tip clearance to the skeg should be at least 12 percent of the diameter. Most other vessels should use 15 percent or greater if at all possible, while high-speed planing craft must have over 20 percent tip clearance. Tip clearance should never be less than 2 inches (50 mm) on any vessel.

For a 30-inch (762 mm) diameter propeller, 15-percent tip clearance is 4.5 inches (114 mm) between hull and blades **[30 in. × 0.15 = 4.5 in.]**.

Insufficient tip clearance is one of the foremost causes of vibration, and frequently, all that is needed to reduce this problem is to switch to a propeller that gives a full 15 to 20 percent tip clearance. If the number of blades is increased to make up for the lost diameter, and a pattern with moderate skew is substituted for non-skewed blades, vibration should be completely eliminated (see Chapter 4).

Fore-and-Aft Blade Clearances

A less-well-known aspect of propeller clearance is the amount of space required fore and aft. Free water flow to the propeller from ahead, and free passage of the water aft as it leaves the propeller is essential for efficiency. It is not unusual to find some vessels, particularly auxiliary sailboats, with propellers in apertures so small that you would have trouble fitting two fingers between the blades and the after end of the deadwood. This is not only terribly inefficient but it can cause a rhythmic thumping every time the propeller blades pass by the deadwood. To avoid this, the skeg or strut should be angled or cut well back from the propeller. (This can be difficult, since the stern bearing ought to be fairly close to the propeller—no more than one to two shaft diameters—for support.

For good performance, though, the skeg or strut should be cut and faired away to leave a gap of at least 30 percent of the propeller diameter at the middle of the propeller blade (at half diameter)—see Figure 7-1. For a 30-inch (762 mm)-diameter propeller, this means that the strut, or aft end of the skeg, should be 9 inches (229 mm) forward of the blades **[30 in. × 0.30 = 9 in.]**—more is better still. In addition, the rudder must be well separated from the propeller. Fifteen percent of diameter is a good average figure.

Figure 7-1

Minimum propeller clearances.

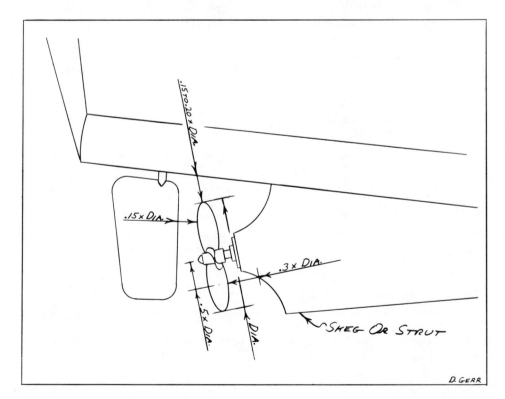

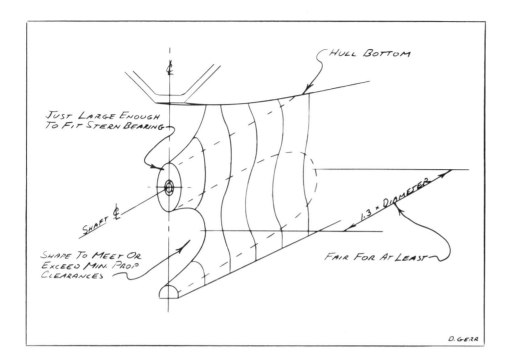

Figure 7-2

Minimum propeller aperture fairing.

Again, for a 30-inch-diameter (762 mm) propeller, the leading edge of the rudder should be at least 4.5 inches (114 mm) aft of the propeller's after hub face **[30 in. × 0.15 = 4.5 in.].** Rudders are more effective if kept fairly close to the propeller—they work best in a concentrated propeller wash—so you should not move the rudder much further aft than this on most craft.

Fairing of Aperture and Struts

Another critical aspect of propeller clearance is the fairing of the deadwood, skeg, or strut. A blunt, square-edge deadwood or strut will create wasteful, turbulent eddies ahead of the propeller, even if cut away from the propeller as called for above. It is vitally important that the trailing edges be faired away as thin as practical in a smooth, gently-rounded curve. (The leading edge of the strut must be well rounded as well.)

Figure 7-2 shows the minimum acceptable fairing on a standard aperture. On wood and GRP vessels, constructing such a faired aperture is relatively straightforward. On metal craft, the designer and builder must use their ingenuity to approximate this shape, within the constraints of reasonable building cost and complexity. One solution is to create a "deadwood" of a vertical centerline plate split for a pipe shaft log, and cut away to the clearances recommended. The trailing edges of the plate at the aperture should be ground to a taper, and the sharp intersection of the pipe and the vertical plate may be filled, rounded and faired with epoxy grout (see Figure 7-3).

Shaft Struts and High-Speed Craft

On twin-screw vessels with vee-struts, it is important that the angle of the vee not match the angle of the propeller blades, which would lead to two blades being masked by the strut simultaneously. Accordingly, on a three-bladed propeller, the angle of the vee should not be 120 degrees, while on a four-bladed propeller, the angle should not be 90 degrees.

On craft that operate at speeds over 35 knots, every effort must be made to fair away the strut and to place it as far ahead of the propeller as possible. A rough rule of thumb for planing craft is that the strut should be 1.5 inches (38 mm) ahead of the propeller for every knot of boat speed. Thus, for a 35-knot craft, the nearest strut ahead of the propeller

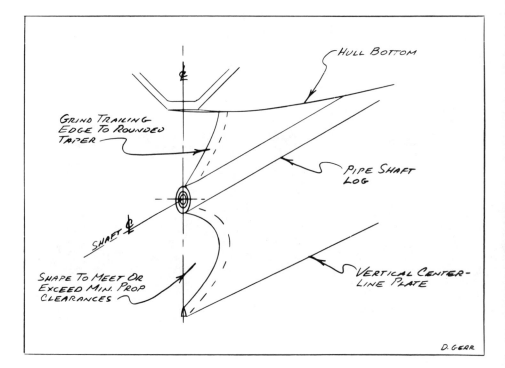

Figure 7-3

Metal propeller aperture.

should be 52.5 inches (1333 mm) away. In practice, this is seldom practical, since the propeller shaft would also have to be supported by a strut just aft of the propeller. Such a strut must be custom-fabricated to include the rudder. This is, in fact, the best practice for racing craft, but it's rarely seen on ordinary vessels, which usually install standard struts just ahead of the propeller and pay the penalty of increased turbulence. Figure 7-4 shows such a high-speed strut, swept well back from the propeller.

SHAFT ANGLE

Shaft Angle Affects Propeller Diameter

In addition to aperture size, shaft angle affects maximum propeller diameter. The steeper the shaft angle for a given engine location, the further below the hull bottom the propeller shaft will emerge from its bearing. Thus, the greater the propeller diameter can be. This is particularly important on twin-screw craft. In a new design, or in any major refit and repowering, some thought should be given to the possibility of increasing diameter by increasing shaft angle, within reasonable limits.

Allowable Limits of Shaft Angle

In theory, a shaft angle of zero—parallel to the waterline—is most efficient, since thrust is straight aft and water flows to the propeller from straight ahead. In practice, it is very difficult to install such a shaft and allow sufficient room for the engine and gearbox inside the hull. Thus, the vast majority of shaft installations fall between 8 and 14 degrees. There is very little difference in performance or efficiency between a shaft angle of 5 and 15 degrees; however, 15 degrees should be taken as an upper limit of shaft angle. Shafts with angles greater than 15 degrees begin to introduce significant variable loading to the propeller blades. This is because the upper blade, as it rotates up, is actually receding from the onrushing water, while the lower blade, as it rotates down, is moving forward into the slipstream. The result is uneven blade loading that can cause vibration and early cavitation.

Shaft Angle in Relation to the Hull's Center of Gravity

On planing vessels, a little-considered aspect of shaft angle is that the shaft line, when extended forward, should pass through or below the center of gravity of the hull—see Figure 7-5. When the shaft line passes through the center of gravity, it tends to drive the vessel straight forward at level trim. When the shaft line passes below the center of gravity the thrust of the propeller tends to lift the bow of the vessel, which—in moderation—is an asset in planing. By contrast, if a shaft is both highly angled and well aft, its thrust line will extend above the vessel's center of gravity, introducing an undesirable bow-down trim. For heavy-displacement vessels these considerations are far less important, although having a shaft line that projects through or below the center of gravity is beneficial.

On a new design, the architect can estimate the fore-and-aft and vertical position of the center of gravity and take it into consideration during the early design stages. On an existing vessel, a major decrease in the shaft angle will usually require relocating the engine, engine beds, shaft log, and stuffing box and all related gear, as well as—usually—forcing the use of a smaller-diameter propeller.

THE PROPELLER SHAFT

Loads on the Propeller Shaft

The propeller shaft does not simply transmit the torque or twisting load of the engine to the propeller. It also carries the entire thrust of the propeller—all the force driving the vessel. Further, as a cantilever beam from the after end of the stern bearing, it supports the weight of the propeller itself. In Chapter 5, we determined the thrust load alone of the relatively small *Svelte Samantha* to be nearly a ton. The thrust on *Ocean Motion*'s shaft is a good 7.5 tons.

Furthermore, the apparently smooth rotary motion of the propeller is not what it seems. Every time a blade swings from the relatively unobstructed water flow in open water, to

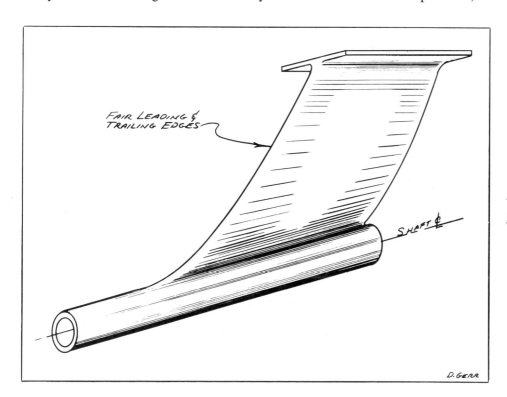

FAIR LEADING &
TRAILING EDGES

SHAFT ₵

D. GERR

Figure 7-4

High-speed propeller strut.

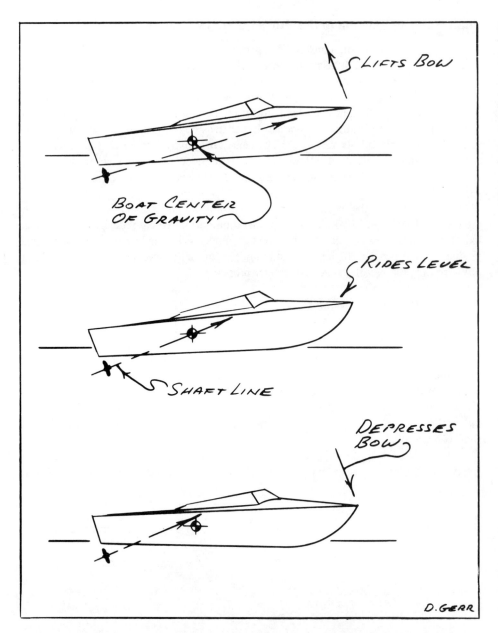

Figure 7-5

Shaft line and trim.

the obstructed water flow behind the strut or deadwood, it changes velocity. Hundredths of a second later, it reenters the unobstructed water flow on the other side of the strut, changing velocity again. As a result, the propeller is actually rotating in powerful little jerks—fits and starts—which add to the strain on the shaft. Of course, while all this is going on, the propeller and the shaft have to withstand the inevitable impacts with floating debris. To accept all these different loads, the propeller shaft must be quite strong.

Propeller or Tail-Shaft Diameter

The One-Fourteenth Diameter Rule   The oldest and simplest rule of thumb for determining propeller shaft diameter is simply that it should be one-fourteenth of the propeller diameter. In spite of its simplicity, this rule works surprisingly well. A 36-inch (914 mm) diameter propeller would require a 2.57-inch (65.3 mm) diameter shaft, by this method.

The one-fourteenth rule, however, does not take into account many of the variables in selecting the best propeller shaft. It does not reflect differences between shaft materials— tobin bronze has roughly 60 percent of the strength of Monel 400, for instance. It also does not directly take into account the many possible combinations of SHP and RPM which dramatically affect torque, though it makes some allowance for this by assuming that the propeller is correctly sized to absorb the engine's power.

In spite of its shortcomings, the one-fourteenth rule should be considered in making a shaft selection, if only for the fact that if a selected shaft diameter varies very widely from the rule, the propeller hub may require special machining.

Determining Propeller-Shaft Diameter Shaft Diameter Chart 7-1 gives the diameter for solid tobin bronze propeller shafts at varying horsepower and RPM. For shafts of Monel 400, the diameter should be reduced by 20 percent. The curves on the chart are derived through the following formula:

Formula 7-1   Shaft Diameter Formula

$$D_s = \sqrt[3]{\frac{321,000 \times SHP \times SF}{St \times RPM}}$$

Where:

D_s = Shaft diameter, in inches

SHP = Shaft horsepower

SF = Safety factor (3 for yachts and light commercial craft, 5 to 8 for heavy commercial craft and racing boats)

St = Yield strength in torsional shear, in PSI

RPM = Revolutions per minute of propeller shaft

Formula 7-1

CHART 7-1   SHAFT DIAMETER

A
10–200 HP : Tobin Bronze

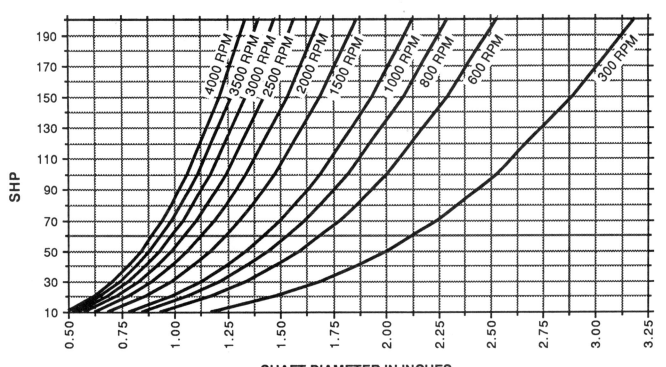

B
200–500 HP : Tobin Bronze

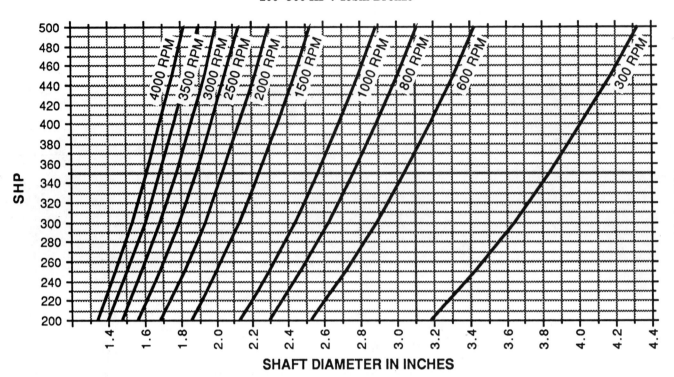

SHAFT DIAMETER IN INCHES

C
500–1,000 HP : Tobin Bronze

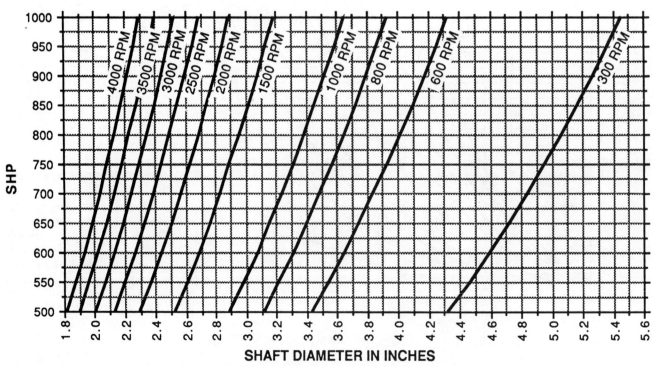

SHAFT DIAMETER IN INCHES

D
1,000–2,000 HP : Tobin Bronze

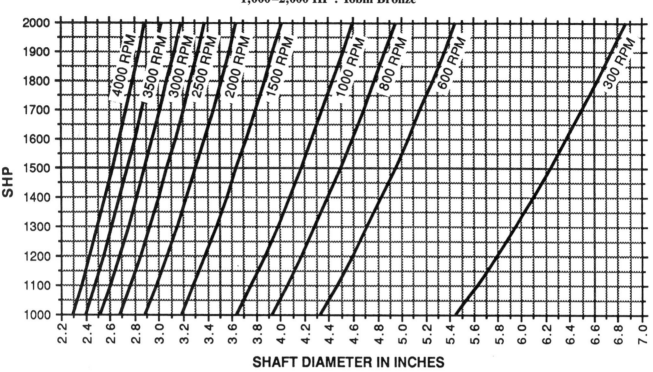

SHAFT DIAMETER IN INCHES

Charts 7-1A, B, C, and D. *These charts, based on Formula 7-1, provide proper diameter for solid tobin bronze propeller shafts at varying horsepowers and RPMs.*

Chart 7-1 uses a safety factor of three—which is most suitable for ordinary service—and the torsional shear strength of tobin bronze from Shaft Material Characteristics Table 7-2. Maximum attainable shaft horsepower and maximum attainable shaft RPM, after the reduction gear, must be used in determining propeller-shaft diameter.

The diameter for shafts of any suitable material and any desired safety factor can be calculated by inserting the appropriate value for the yield strength of that material and the desired value for safety factor in Formula 7-1.

TABLE 7-2 SHAFT MATERIAL CHARACTERISTICS

Shaft Material	Yield Strength in Torsional Shear, PSI	Modulus of Elasticity, PSI	Density lb./cu. in.
Aquamet 22	70,000	28,000,000	0.285
Aquamet 18	60,000	28,800,000	0.281
Aquamet 17	70,000	28,500,000	0.284
Monel 400	40,000	26,000,000	0.319
Monel K500	67,000	26,000,000	0.306
Tobin Bronze	20,000	16,000,000	0.304
Stainless Steel 304	20,000	28,000,000	0.286

TABLE 7-2

High-Strength Alloys for Propeller Shafting Aquamet 22, 18, and 17, manufactured by the Armco Steel Corp., and Monel 400 and K500, manufactured by the International

Nickel Company, offer the highest strengths and best corrosion characteristics of all available shaft materials. Since shafts made of these alloys can have smaller diameters, their cost is not significantly greater than for ordinary tobin bronze shafts, and these materials should be employed in all heavy commercial vessels and racing boats. For ordinary small craft and light commercial vessels, tobin, manganese, or silicone bronze or NAB bronze shafting is quite adequate, though cathodic protection against corrosion may be necessary.

Reduced Diameter for Intermediate Shafts   Where the propeller shaft is divided into a tail shaft that supports the propeller and an intermediate shaft or shafts, the intermediate shafts may be only 95 percent of the diameter of the tail shaft. (Chart 7-1 and Formula 7-1 give the tail-shaft diameter.)

Shaft Diameter for Ocean Motion   Using Shaft Diameter Chart 7-1 or Formula 7-1 for *Ocean Motion*—our example from Chapter 6—with a maximum SHP of 1,020 HP (760 kw) and 360 shaft RPM, we come up with a tobin bronze shaft 5.16 inches (131 mm) in diameter, or a Monel 400 shaft 4.13 inches (105 mm) in diameter. The propeller selected for *Ocean Motion* was 74 inches (1879 mm) in diameter, so the one-fourteenth rule gives a shaft diameter of 5.28 inches (134 mm). This checks well with the calculated size of the tobin bronze shaft, but fails to give accurate results with stronger materials like Monel or Aquamet alloys.

Shaft Bearings

The Twenty-Times—Forty-Times Bearing Spacing Rule   The simplest rule of thumb for determining shaft-bearing spacing is that the bearings should be no closer together than twenty times the shaft diameter, and no further apart than forty times the shaft diameter. This rule is less reliable than the one-fourteenth rule for propeller shaft selection, and it should be used as a rough guide only. Very frequently, bearing spacing is considerably more than forty times the shaft diameter. Additional bearings simply add expense and unwanted shaft rigidity.

Determining Shaft-Bearing Spacing   The propeller shaft must be supported by intermediate shaft bearings—pillow blocks—between the flange coupling at the engine or gearbox and the stern bearing, unless the shaft is relatively short in proportion to its diameter. Chart 7-2 gives the maximum spacing between shaft bearings for propeller shafts with flexible bearings at both ends. Most small craft have a rigid bearing at the engine and a rigid stern bearing, just ahead of the propeller. Such shafts should have maximum bearing spacings 50 percent greater than that given on the chart.

Figure 7-6

Typical shaft installation showing propeller with fairing over nut, propeller strut and stern bearing, shaft coupling, self-aligning stuffing box, and flexible shaft coupling.

(Courtesy of W.H. Den Ouden Vetus)

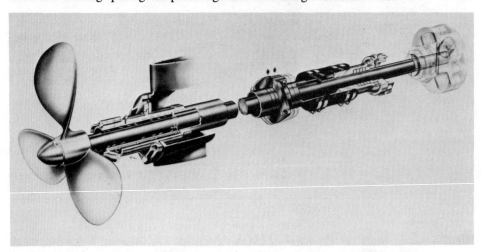

CHART 7-2   SHAFT-BEARING SPACING

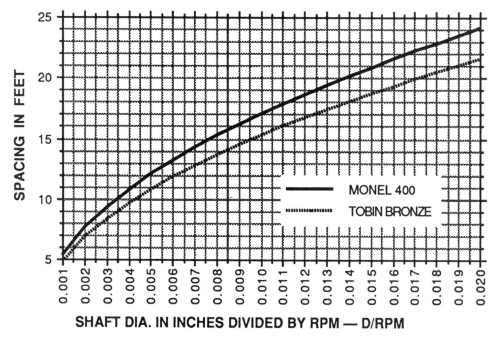

SHAFT DIA. IN INCHES DIVIDED BY RPM — D/RPM

Chart 7-2. *This chart, based on Formula 7-2, depicts recommended shaft bearing spacing for Monel 400 and tobin bronze. Values for other metals may be substituted in the formula.*

The curves on Chart 7-2 are based on the following formula:

Formula 7-2   Shaft-Bearing Spacing Formula

$$Ft = \sqrt{\frac{3.21 \times D_s}{RPM}} \times \sqrt[4]{\frac{E}{Dens}}$$

Where:

Ft = Shaft-bearing spacing, in feet

D_s = Propeller shaft diameter, in inches

RPM = Propeller shaft speed, in revolutions per minute

E = Modulus of elasticity of shaft material, in PSI

Dens = Density of shaft material, in pounds per cubic inch

Formula 7-2

The modulus of elasticity (E) and the density for tobin bronze and Monel 400 from Table 7-2 were used to generate the curves on Chart 7-2. Values for other suitable shaft materials may be substituted in Formula 7-2.

It is important that the propeller shaft be able to flex slightly to accommodate the flexing under strain of the entire hull. For this reason, shaft-bearing spacing should be no closer than necessary and the shaft diameter should be no larger than required.

For *Ocean Motion,* with a Monel 400 shaft 4.13 inches (105 mm) in diameter and a maximum shaft speed of 360 RPM, Dia/RPM is 0.0115. Therefore, from Chart 7-2 or Formula 7-2, her shaft bearings should be spaced 18.2 feet (5.5 m) apart. If *Ocean Motion's* shaft were one-piece, continuous and held at a rigid bearing at the engine and at the stern bearing, the correct shaft spacing would be 50 percent greater, or 27.3 feet (8.3 m).

CHART 7-3 ESTIMATING PROPELLER WEIGHT

18–54 Inches

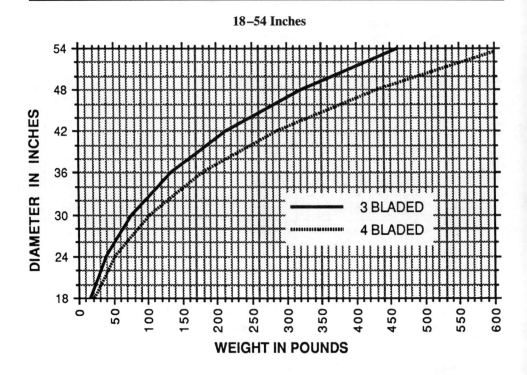

54–96 Inches

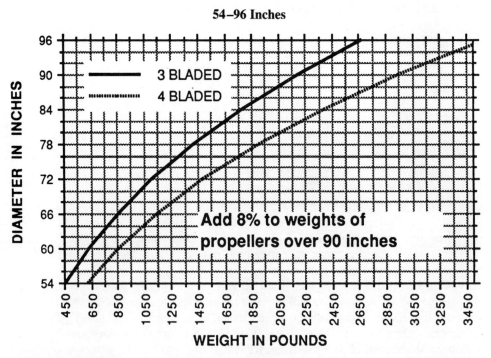

Charts 7-3A and B. *Approximate weight of standard bronze three- and four-bladed propellers, of 0.33 mean-width ratio and 20-percent hub diameter, plotted against propeller diameter. Derived from Formulas 7-3a and b.*

PROPELLER WEIGHTS

It is frequently helpful to be able to estimate the weight of a propeller in advance, whether for weight or structural calculations, or in preparing for installation. The weights for propellers of similar pattern increase at just over the cube of the increase in their diameters. Chart 7-3 plots the approximate weight of standard bronze three- and four-bladed propellers, of 0.33 mean width ratio and 20 percent hub diameter, against overall diameter. The weights given in this chart are approximate, but fall within 10 percent of actual weight. For propellers over 90 inches in diameter, add another 8 percent to account for the increased scantlings required for the higher proportionate bending moments on these propellers.

Chart 7-3 is based on the following formulas, derived by the author:

Propeller Weight Estimate Formulas:

Formula 7-3a Three-Bladed Propeller Weight

$$Wgt = 0.00241 \times D^{3.05}$$

Formula 7-3b   Four-Bladed Propeller Weight

$$Wgt = 0.00323 \times D^{3.05}$$

Where:

Wgt = Weight of propeller in pounds

D = Diameter of propeller in inches

Formula 7-3a,b

From Chart 7-3 or Formula 7-3, *Ocean Motion*'s three-bladed, 74-inch (1879 mm) propeller would weigh approximately 1,210 pounds (549 kg), while *Svelte Samantha*'s three-bladed, 26-inch (660 mm) propeller would weigh around 50 pounds (23 kg).

Chapter 8
Tugs and Trawlers

High-Thrust, Variable-Loading;
Controllable-Pitch; and Ducted Propellers

TUGBOATS

Nature of Variable Loading on Tugs

Selecting a suitable fixed-pitch propeller for a tugboat is a difficult task. As we have seen, the pitch of the propeller can only be exactly right for one set of operating conditions. By the very nature of its work, however, a tug operates under vastly differing conditions—from turning the head of a large liner or tanker, to towing a barge train, to running free between jobs. By contrast, most other vessels have fairly constant operating requirements.

A Fixed-Pitch Propeller Must Be a Compromise

Because of these widely varying operating conditions, selecting the correct propeller—particularly the one with the best pitch—is always a major compromise. Smaller tugs that tow relatively large and heavy loads will operate at relatively lower speeds than larger tugs pushing proportionately smaller loads. The smaller tug will do better with proportionately less pitch than the larger, faster one, yet neither vessel would be fitted with the pitch required for maximum efficiency at maximum free-running speed. Of course, since all tugboats operate at relatively low speeds and require high thrust, the one primary concern is to use the largest diameter propeller and the slowest shaft RPM practical.

Even choosing the correct power for a tug is more difficult than for ordinary, free-running craft. The speed and power formulas in Chapter 2 will not help to determine the speed of a tug when towing. Even a detailed analysis of the resistance of a tow is nearly useless. One day a tug may be pushing a heavily loaded barge train inshore, the next day it may be running unloaded barges offshore, and the following day it may assist a ship to dock. There is little point in calculating exact tow resistance since it varies so dramatically in every job and condition.

Estimating Horsepower and Towing Speed for Tugs

Charts 8-1, 8-2, and 8-3 will give good guidance in selecting suitable power for tugs and estimating their average towing speed (V) in knots. Chart 8-1 gives minimum average brake horsepower for standard harbor and coastal tugs of between 60 and 150 feet (18.3 to 45.7 m) in length overall. Since shorter tugs are more maneuverable than longer ones, there has been a trend to increasing BHP above the values on this chart to get more tow power in a smaller, handier craft. In addition, in recent years some offshore tugs have had nearly 70 percent more BHP installed than suggested in Chart 8-1. Accordingly, in selecting an engine, one should usually round up to the nearest appropriate size. The curve in Chart 8-1 is based on the following formula, derived by the author:

Formula 8-1   Brake Horsepower vs LOA Formula—Tugs

BHP = 100 + (LOA$^{4.15}$ ÷ 111,000)

Where:

BHP = Maximum brake horsepower of engine

LOA = Length overall of the tug, in feet.

Formula 8-1

CHART 8-1   BRAKE HORSEPOWER VS LOA—TUGS

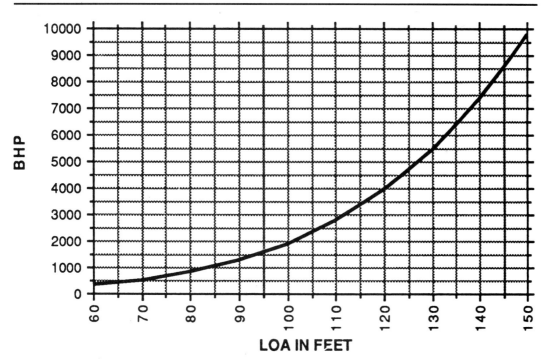

Chart 8-1. *This chart, related to Formula 8-1, gives minimum average brake horsepower for standard harbor and coastal tugs of between 60 and 150 feet in length.*

Chart 8-2 gives the average towing speed (V) in knots of a standard tug towing an average load. It assumes that the LOA of the tug is within 15 to 20 percent of the values given in Chart 8-1. Chart 8-2 is based on the following formula, derived by the author:

Formula 8-2   Towing Speed vs Brake Horsepower

Kts = 1.43 × BHP$^{0.21}$

Where:

Kts = Average speed in knots during an average tow

BHP = Maximum brake horsepower of engine

Formula 8-2

Chart 8-3 gives the average, high, and low values of barges towed in deadweight tons (DWT). The average line, obviously, represents the average capacity in average conditions. The high DWT line represents the maximum DWT that can usually be towed with this BHP in fair inshore conditions. If the tows contemplated will consistently fall below the level of the low DWT line, then the engine—and probably the tug itself—is too large for economical operation in the intended service.

CHART 8-2   TOWING SPEED VS BRAKE HORSEPOWER—TUGS

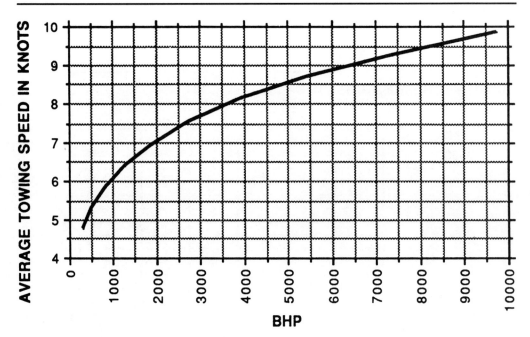

Chart 8-2. *Average towing speed in knots of a standard tug towing an average load. From*
362   *Formula 8-2.*

CHART 8-3   WEIGHTS OF BARGES TOWED VS BHP—TUGS

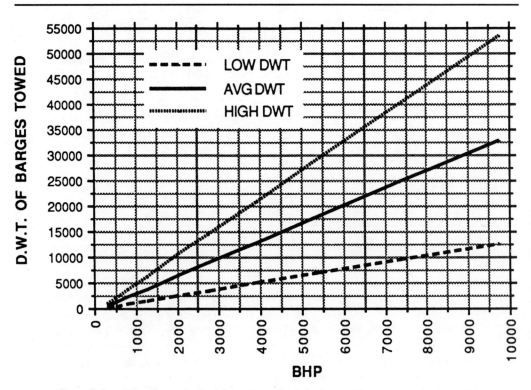

Chart 8-3. *This chart, derived from Formula 8-3, depicts the average, high, and low sizes
of barges against the brake horsepower required to handle them.*

The curves on Chart 8-3 are based on the following formulas, derived by the author:

D.W.T. of Barges Towed vs BHP Formulas:

Formula 8-3a

Low DWT = $(1.32 \times BHP) - 255.25$

Formula 8-3b

Avg DWT = $(3.43 \times BHP) - 599.18$

Formula 8-3c

High DWT = $(5.57 \times BHP) - 943.10$
Where:
DWT = Deadweight tons of barges towed
BHP = Maximum brake horsepower of engine

Formula 8-3a,b,c

A Sample Tug Calculation—Tenacious Teddy

Let's find the best compromise propeller for our single-screw, 92.5-foot (28.18 m) tug, *Tenacious Teddy*. Her characteristics are as follows:

Tenacious Teddy		
92.5 ft.	28.18 m	LOA (length overall)
85.4 ft.	26.03 m	LWL (length waterline)
25 ft.	7.62 m	BOA (beam overall)
24 ft.	7.31 m	BWL (beam waterline)
11 ft.	3.34 m	Hd (hull draft)
11.8 ft.	3.59 m	Maximum draft
287 tons	291 Mtons	Displacement (long tons, metric tons)
642,000 lb	291206 kg	Displacement (pounds, kilograms)
0.45	0.45	Cb (block coefficient)
106 in.	269 cm	Maximum propeller diameter to fit within existing aperture
5.6 ft.	1.71 m	Shaft centerline below waterline

From Chart 8-1 or Formula 8-1, we find that an average tug 92.5 feet (28.18 m) LOA would use around a 1,500 BHP (1118 kw) engine. Inspection of manufacturers' literature shows that a Caterpillar 3516-V16 continuous-duty marine diesel delivers 1,710 BHP (1275 kw) at 1,800 RPM, which would be suitable for our purpose. With a tug's large reduction gear and heavy bearings, we will allow for a 7 percent loss of BHP. This gives us a SHP (shaft horsepower) of 1,590 (1185 kw).

Entering DIA-HP-RPM Formula 5-3, with 1,590 SHP (1185 kw) and 106 inches (269 cm) maximum diameter, we come up with a preliminary shaft speed of 234 RPM. This requires a 7.86:1 reduction ratio. The nearest commercially available ratio is 8.0:1, which yields 225 RPM.

We can now enter the BP-δ charts at the end of Chapter 6 to calculate the propeller.

We must do at least two calculations, though—one for towing conditions and one for free running. The first is the most crucial, since it is the towing conditions that will generate the highest blade loading and thus determine the minimum acceptable developed blade area.

The Towing-Screw Calculation From Chart 8-2 or Formula 8-2, we find that average towing speed will be around 6.8 knots. Wake Factor vs Block Coefficient Formula 6-4a gives a single-screw wake factor (Wf), with our Cb of 0.45, of 0.84. Thus, the towing Va will be approximately 5.7 knots.

From Bp and δ Formulas 6-7 and 6-8, we find that Bp equals 115.7 and δ equals 348.7. Trying a three-bladed, 0.50 DAR propeller first, we find that the theoretical maximum open water δ would be 405; with the single-screw adjustment factor of 0.95 from Table 6-2, we get an adjusted δ of 384.7. This δ means that our 106-inch (269 cm) diameter propeller is a bit smaller than the ideal size of 116.9 inches (297 cm). Unfortunately, though, we do not have the space to install a bigger propeller on *Tenacious Teddy*.

Taking the δ of 348.7 for the largest propeller we can use (106 inches), and multiplying by the single-screw adjustment of 0.95, we get a usable adjusted δ of 331.3. Reading across on the Bp diagram from the pitch ratio side, we find a pitch ratio of 0.85, or a 90-inch (229 cm) pitch. Efficiency (η) crosses Bp of 115.7 and δ of 331.3 at 0.38. Developed blade area (Ad) from Formula 4-6 for a 106-inch (269 cm) diameter, three-bladed propeller of 0.50 DAR is 4,453 square inches (28730 cm²).

We can now check blade loading. Formula 5-6 shows the maximum allowable blade loading as 5.2 PSI (35849 N/m²), while Actual Blade Loading Formula 5-7 yields 7.7 PSI (53084 N/m²), which is too high. We must use a propeller with a greater blade area. Solving Formula 5-7 for the required blade area shows that we need 6,650 square inches (42906 cm²), and using Formula 4-6, we find that a four-bladed propeller of 0.75 DAR would give us the area we need.

The highest DAR diagram we have for a four-blader is for a DAR of 0.55. We'll use this and adjust for loss of efficiency with Table 6-3. Entering Bp-δ Chart 6-4c with a Bp of 115 and an adjusted δ of 331.3, we find that we should use a pitch ratio of 0.80, for a pitch of 84.8 inches (215 cm). Efficiency is found to be 0.38; however, we have to adjust for the additional blade area of our wide blades. Interpolating from Table 6-3, we find that efficiency should be 93 percent of our presently calculated propeller, which gives an efficiency of 0.35. Thus, the best propeller we could select for towing conditions is a four-blader, 106 inches (269 cm) in diameter, with an 84-inch (213 cm) pitch, a 0.75 DAR and a 0.37 MWR, and with a hub about 20 percent of diameter. Unfortunately, this is not also the best propeller for maximum speed running free.

The Free-Running Calculation Since we cannot have ideal pitch for both running free and towing, we have to select one or the other, or compromise between the two. Usually it's best to select pitch for the lowest acceptable free-running speed and take the inevitable loss of thrust while towing. In the case of *Tenacious Teddy*, we will settle on a free-running speed of 11 knots, or a speed-length ratio of 1.2.

We must now reenter Chart 6-4c for the propeller pattern we have selected, with the Bp and δ values for a V of 11 knots. Accordingly, Va becomes 9.24; Bp, 34.6; and δ, 215. The adjusted δ is now 204. Reading from the diagram, we get a new free-running pitch ratio of 0.92, for a pitch of 97.5 inches (248 cm). Efficiency (η) is found to be 0.53, and adjusted by 93 percent for the increased blade area of our pattern, η is 0.49. Thus, for free running at 11 knots, we select a four-bladed propeller 106 inches (269 cm) in diameter, 98 inches (249 cm) in pitch, and with a 0.75 DAR, a 0.37 MWR, and a hub about 20 percent of diameter. We could use narrower blades and less area for free running alone, but we have already determined that we need this additional area to avoid excessive blade loading and cavitation when towing.

Loss of Thrust During Towing with the Free-Running Screw   We should now check to see how much thrust we have lost at towing speed with this higher-pitch propeller. Entering our free-running pitch ratio of 0.92 and reading at the intersection with the towing Bp of 115, we find a δ of 323 during towing. This intersects efficiency at 0.36, and making the 93 percent reduction for efficiency for our wider blades, we get a towing η of 0.33. The lower-pitch, all-towing propeller had an η of 0.35, giving a ratio of 94 percent [0.33 ÷ 0.35 = 0.94]. Accordingly, the higher-pitch, free-running propeller will deliver only 94 percent of the thrust of the ideal towing propeller. This is an acceptable compromise.

Finally, we determine maximum thrust towing from Thrust Formula 5-8 (using the free-running propeller we will actually install) and find it to be 13.4 long tons. Bollard pull or static thrust, from Formula 5-9, is 16.8 long tons. It's important to note that if we had had room to install the optimum 116-inch (297 cm) diameter propeller, bollard pull would have been 17.8 long tons—an increase of 6 percent. If *Tenacious Teddy* were a new design, it would be well worth modifying the lines and engine placement to accommodate this additional diameter.

CONTROLLABLE-PITCH PROPELLERS

The Solution to Variable Loading Conditions

There is a very simple solution to the problem of matching pitch to variable loading conditions—install a controllable-pitch propeller. As we mentioned in Chapter 4, this type of propeller allows the operator to twist or rotate each propeller blade about the blade axis during operation. As a result, the pitch can be changed at will to exactly suit prevailing conditions.

Selecting a Controllable-Pitch Propeller

Although the design and construction of a controllable-pitch propeller is complex, selecting one is quite easy. Diameter is found exactly the same way as for a standard fixed-pitch propeller using either Chart 5-3 or Formula 5-3, or the Bp and δ factors contained in Chart 6-4. That is it. Since pitch is fully controllable, no pitch calculation need be done. It's wise to consult with the manufacturer of the propeller before final installation for suggestions as to sizing, shafting and the pitch-control mechanism.

Pitch controls can be direct, manually-operated mechanical linkages, electrically operated mechanical linkages, or hydraulic systems. The primary difference between these pitch controls is complexity and cost. All will give good service, with one exception. Hydraulic controls should never be used on motorsailers and sailboats. This is because the pressure in the hydraulic system is somewhat dependent on engine power, and it may not be sustained at the low engine RPMs and powers at which these vessels often cruise.

Avoiding Engine Overload

A further consideration with controllable-pitch propellers is that there is the possibility of overloading the engine. If, for example, the throttle is set at maximum, and additional pitch is cranked into the blades, the engine will be overloaded and lug down. This causes a dangerous rise in engine temperature and oil pressure, and can ruin a good engine quickly. To avoid this, fit an oil-pressure alarm. Tugs and trawlers with highly variable loading should also consider installing a pyrometer (high-temperature thermometer) in the exhaust just aft of the manifold to detect significant rises in operating temperature quickly. Some manufacturers offer automatic pitch-adjustment control, governed by the rise and fall in oil pressure.

Figure 8-1

Typical three-bladed, controllable-pitch propeller with shaft coupling and pitch-control mechanism. In this case, pitch is adjusted manually via the wheel; however, remote control mechanical and hydraulic linkages are also commonly employed.

(Courtesy of Scandinavian Propellers a/s)

Types of Controllable-Pitch Propellers

Because of the practical limits on blade rotation, controllable-pitch propellers are generally available in one of three configurations.

- Adjustable pitch only (no reverse pitch).
- Adjustable pitch with full reverse pitch, going right through fully neutral pitch (blades at right angles to the water flow, so the propeller can rotate at full speed without generating thrust or absorbing power). Such propellers eliminate the need for a reverse gear, and enable the vessel to go from full ahead to full astern without changing the direction of shaft rotation.
- Fully feathering but not reversible. This arrangement allows the blades to line up exactly fore-and-aft so they give minimum resistance to the water flow. These propellers are ideal for motorsailers and sailboats, but have little application on most other vessels.

Drawbacks of Controllable-Pitch Propellers

There are two reasons why controllable-pitch propellers are not more common. The first—and most important—is their high cost. Not only do they cost much more than a standard fixed-pitch propeller to begin with, but the complex control mechanism must be carefully maintained throughout the life of the vessel. The second reason is that controllable-pitch propellers are generally not as efficient in reverse as comparable fixed-pitch propellers. For tugs, which need to be able to exert high thrust both ahead and astern, this can be a significant drawback. Further, the pitch of a controllable-pitch propeller forms a true helix (constant pitch) at only one pitch setting. As the blades are rotated away from this one angle, their pitch varies, causing uneven blade loading and some loss of efficiency. In spite of these disadvantages, controllable-pitch propellers are being employed on more and more vessels of every class.

Figure 8-2

Dimension drawing of a typical three-bladed, controllable-pitch propeller showing shaft coupling and pitch-control mechanism.

(Courtesy of Scandinavian Propellers a/s)

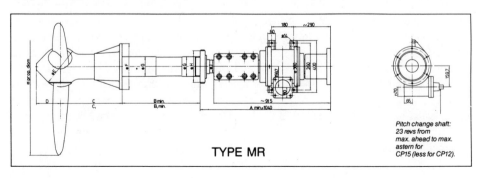

TYPE MR

Pitch change shaft: 23 revs from max. ahead to max. astern for CP15 (less for CP12).

DUCTED PROPELLERS OR KORT NOZZLES

Describing a Ducted Propeller

Kort nozzles or ducted propellers are propellers surrounded with a hydrodynamically shaped ring or shroud (see Figure 8-3). The shroud fits very closely around the propeller blade tips and is specifically designed to accelerate water flow through the propeller.

The propeller itself, inside the duct or nozzle, has square tips—very much like a standard elliptical blade cut off at about 70 percent of diameter. The most common of these blades are the Kaplan-accelerating series. These are available in three- , four- and five-bladed propellers of various disc area ratios—the most common being four-bladed, with DARs of 0.55 and 0.70. Close tip clearances are not a problem for ducted propellers because there is no difference in clearance throughout the passage of the blade. This avoids detrimental changes in pressure, as there would be if a blade swept close to the hull and then away into open water (see Chapter 7).

Increased Efficiency with Ducted Propellers

Ducted propellers offer a significant increase in efficiency over standard open propellers, but *only* under special conditions. A rough rule of thumb is that the vessel be intended to operate at or under 12 knots. A more exact measure is the power coefficient (Bp). Bp *must* be greater than 25 for ducted propellers to offer any advantage at all. For a significant advantage, Bp must be greater than 30. If Bp values are 35 or over, an increase in propeller towing power of about 30 percent over a standard four-bladed, DAR-0.70 propeller (at the same SHP and RPM) will be found. At lower Bp values, or speeds higher than 12 knots, the additional drag of the nozzle will far outweigh the increase in thrust.

Intended Use of Nozzles

Nozzles come in a number of shapes designed to meet specific performance requirements. The most significant variables are between nozzles designed for optimum ahead operation only, and nozzles designed for both ahead and astern thrust.

Controllable-Pitch Propellers and Nozzles

Controllable-pitch propellers also may be fitted in nozzles. This combination offers the maximum possible thrust at all speed and loading conditions for vessels that operate at speeds suited to nozzles. The drawback is that controllable-pitch propeller blades of optimum diameter cannot rotate from ahead through astern, because this would cause the blade tips to jam against the inside of the shroud. Accordingly, a reverse gear must be fitted with such systems.

Increase in Bollard Pull with Ducted Propellers

The lower the boat speed, the greater the gain in thrust. Table 8-1 gives approximate relative bollard pulls for varying configurations.

TABLE 8-1   NOZZLE BOLLARD PULL

	Standard Propeller	Ahead Only	Ahead & Astern	
Ahead Pull	1.00	1.40	1.38	*TABLE 8-1*
Astern Pull	0.79	0.80	1.10	

All bollard pulls are related to the ahead pull of a standard, four-bladed open propeller of 0.70 DAR, with about a 6-percent-greater diameter than the nozzle propeller. You can

Figure 8-3

A ducted propeller installation. In this case, the duct or shroud is a bit longer fore-and-aft than standard, and the entire duct swings or steers to direct thrust.

(Courtesy of The Michigan Wheel Company)

see that very significant increases in low-speed thrust are possible with the nozzle propeller. For most vessels, a nozzle designed for optimum ahead only operation is appropriate. For tugs, however, nozzles designed for both ahead and astern operation should be installed.

Additional Advantages of Ducted Propellers

In addition to increasing thrust, ducted propellers can increase fuel efficiency. Installing a nozzle on an existing vessel, for example, will enable her to run at lower RPM while attaining the same speed as before. This can amount to an 8 to 10 percent savings in fuel cost. Alternatively, a ducted-propeller system will allow the same engine, operating at the same RPM, to increase towing speed by 10 to 15 percent.

Tenacious Teddy, with her free running Bp of 34.6, towing Bp of 115, and top speed of 11 knots, is an ideal candidate for a nozzle. With such an installation, an approximate 30-percent increase in tow-speed thrust can be expected. Thus the tug's towing thrust would increase to 17.4 long tons, and her bollard pull, from Table 8-1, would jump to around 23.2 long tons. These values can be determined more exactly by referring to the Bp-δ chart from the manufacturer for the particular pattern of nozzle and propeller being installed and using the standard Bp-δ propeller selection method.

Maneuverability with a Ducted Propeller System

A nozzle installed without alteration to the rudder and steering system will increase the turning circle or tactical diameter of a vessel by about 20 percent. By contrast, a ducted propeller may be fitted with a system of two or three rudders very close astern of, or mated to, the nozzle. Such a rudder system directs the concentrated propeller wash from the aft end of the nozzle, and can allow very high rudder angles (50 to 60 degrees, as opposed to 30 to 40 degrees for a conventional rudder). When properly designed, this type of system gives significant improvement in handling. The turning circle can be reduced by as much as 60 to 70 percent from that of a standard open propeller and single rudder.

It is critical that the nozzle system manufacturer be consulted before the final design and installation of a nozzle or ducted propeller system, both to obtain the appropriate Bp-δ diagrams, and to ensure that the nozzle installation will actually fit in the available space.

STEERABLE Z-DRIVE SYSTEMS

The ultimate in maneuverability is obtained from steerable drive systems. These systems are essentially Z-drives that allow full 360-degree rotation about the vertical shaft line. Accordingly, thrust may be directed in any direction at will, very much like an outboard—although outboards, of course, are more limited in their direction of rotation.

These drives are sometimes known as Schottle Drives, after the Schottle Company which was one of their pioneers. Another steerable Z-drive is the Aquamaster, made by Hollming Ltd. Figure 8-4 shows a section through an Aquamaster drive fitted with a nozzle. Steerable Z-drives are available with or without nozzles, and some may be installed at the stern of the vessel with the ability to kick up just like a small outboard or inboard-outboard. For commercial vessels operating at under 14 knots or so, where maneuverability is the number-one consideration, steerable Z-drives are the ultimate solution.

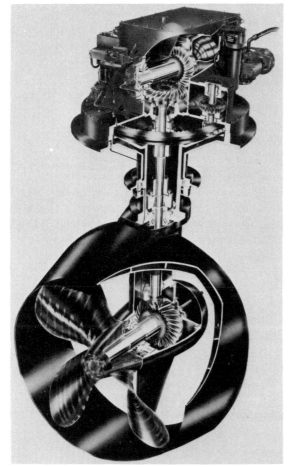

Figure 8-4

Cutaway view of a steerable Z-drive with a duct or shroud installed at the propeller.

(Courtesy of Aquamaster-Ruma Ltd.)

TRAWLERS

In many respects, the requirements of a trawler are very similar to those of a tugboat. Like tugs, trawlers operate under conditions of widely varying load and speed. And, as with a tug, a trawler's fixed-pitch propeller must be calculated for both towing or trawling conditions, and for free running. A compromise propeller based on the lowest acceptable free-running speed, and with sufficient blade area to avoid cavitation with trawling, can then be selected.

Trawl Speed and Power

Trawling speeds are usually between 5 and 7 knots, depending on the size of the vessel and the nature of the trawl. Trawlers, though, do not have to install nearly the power that tugs do. Displacement Speed Chart 2-1 or Formula 2-1 may be applied. Use the minimum acceptable free-running speed and add 6 to 8 percent to the SHP indicated.

Controllable-Pitch and Ducted Propellers for Trawlers

Controllable-pitch propellers can eliminate the necessity of compromising on pitch, just as with tugs. The savings from decreased fuel costs and increased free-running speed frequently can more than pay back the higher initial and maintenance costs of a controllable-pitch propeller. Similarly, most trawlers operate at speeds where ducted propellers will improve efficiency and thrust. The nozzle or shroud also has the beneficial side effect of somewhat reducing the chance of the trawl or associated gear fouling the propeller.

Chapter 9
Sailboats, Outboards, and Go-Fast Wrinkles

Propellers for Special Applications

In this chapter we will examine the requirements of two very different types of vessels—sailboats that operate at low speed and often place secondary importance on their propeller installations, and inboard- and inboard-outboard boats with their high-speed installation requirements and techniques.

PROPELLERS FOR SAILBOATS AND MOTORSAILERS

The Need for Reduced Propeller Drag Under Sail

Sailing vessels equipped with engines range from light-displacement racing craft to performance cruisers to heavy-displacement motorsailers. With regard to their propellers, however, they all have one thing in common—the need to combine reduced propeller drag under sail with adequate propeller thrust under power.

Approaches to Reducing Drag

There are just two fundamental ways to achieve a reduction in drag, and whenever possible, both approaches should be used together:

- Make the propeller blades and blade area as small as possible.
- Hide the propeller behind the keel or deadwood.

The first approach also has a number of secondary possibilities:

1. Use a solid, two-bladed propeller with narrow blades (usually with a MWR of about 0.21 and a DAR of around 0.24).
2. Fold the two blades flat against each other when under sail (the folding propeller).
3. Without folding the blades, turn them so that they align straight fore-and-aft (the feathering propeller).

Advantages and Disadvantages of Approaches to Reduced Drag

Generally, for a given diameter and shaft RPM, the folding propeller offers the least drag under sail and gives the lowest thrust under power. For cruising sailboats, feathering propellers usually offer the best combination of low drag under sail and good thrust under power. This is because the blades can effectively be made larger than those of most folding propellers, giving better blade-loading and thrust characteristics. A fixed two- or three-bladed propeller, in the open, produces the most drag under sail, and yet its thrust under power is hardly better than that of a good two- or three-bladed feathering propeller.

On cruising vessels, with the propeller hidden in an aperture behind the deadwood, a *fixed* two-blader can be locked vertically in the aperture and thus largely kept out of the slipstream around the keel. This is a good, reliable and inexpensive solution for non-performance craft. Note, though, that a two-bladed *feathering* propeller, while producing virtually the same thrust under power, will, when locked vertically in the same aperture, create significantly less drag under sail.

Locked Propeller or Free to Rotate for Minimum Drag?

This brings us to the old argument as to whether a propeller produces the least drag when it is free to rotate or locked. The answer is both, depending on the configuration of the hull, keel and propeller. (Note, though, that some gearboxes are not lubricated unless the engine is running; if so, their bearings will be destroyed if the shaft is allowed to rotate.) If the propeller is neither folding nor feathering, and is exposed to the water flow—as with a propeller on a strut well aft of a fin keel—it will generate the least drag when it is free to rotate. If, on the other hand, a fixed two-blader can be well hidden behind the keel, it will produce less drag when locked vertically. Fully-feathering propellers should be locked vertically, if possible, while folding propellers need not be locked since they show so little area and have no tendency to rotate when folded.

Folding and Feathering Mechanisms

Both folding propellers and feathering propellers rely on centrifugal force or the torque of the propeller shaft to open them, and on the pressure of the water—when under power—to hold them open. The force of the water pushes them closed, when the propeller shaft is not rotating and there is no thrust, once the speed of the vessel exceeds 1½ knots or so. Early versions of folding and feathering propellers allowed the blades to fold or pivot more or less independently. Although many of these designs are still on the market, they offer less-than-satisfactory service. The blades can open and close out of step with each other and, on folders, the lower blade will often hang down in an annoying fashion under sail.

The solution to these problems has been to put geared connections between the blade and the closing mechanism on folding or feathered propellers. The best of these propellers open and close evenly and positively, and their additional cost is small compared to the gain in efficiency and control.

Figure 9-1

A two-bladed feathering propeller in fully feathered position has a remarkably low-drag shape.

(Courtesy of PYI Inc.)

Figure 9-2

When in use, a three-bladed feathering propeller delivers almost as much thrust as a fixed three-blader, while in the fully feathered position, it creates less drag than a fixed two-bladed propeller.

(Courtesy of PYI Inc.)

Feathering Propellers

To reduce folded frontal area to a minimum, most feathering propellers have flat blades with no built-in twist for true helical or constant pitch. As a result, even with the same blade area as a fixed-bladed propeller, they cannot be as efficient. It's interesting that a feathering propeller can actually be more efficient than a fixed-bladed propeller when in reverse. This is because the feathering blades will pivot so that their leading edges always face into the direction of rotation, while fixed blades, obviously, cannot.

For larger cruising vessels, where even greater thrust under power is required, a three-bladed feathering propeller is an ideal solution. When feathered, such a propeller will produce no more drag than most fixed two-bladers, and yet it will deliver as much as 90 percent of the ahead thrust of a fixed three-blader. A further refinement in the best feathering propellers is the ability to adjust the pitch. When powering begins, a feathering propeller goes from fully feathered to fully open, immediately. When fully open, its blades will be at a given pitch. By controlling how far open the blades can go, the pitch of the propeller can be adjusted to exactly suit each installation. It is necessary to haul the boat in order to adjust the pitch, though.

Folding Propellers for Performance Craft

Owners of racing craft or performance cruisers often find even the reduced drag of a good feathering propeller excessive. The answer then is to turn to a geared folding propeller. Since the blades on these propellers are made as narrow as possible, the blade shape that

TWO BLADE   THREE BLADE

Figure 9-3

Diagrams of the feathering mechanisms of the two- and three-bladed propellers shown in Figures 9-1 and 9-2. Both of these propellers allow pitch adjustments.

(Courtesy of PYI Inc.)

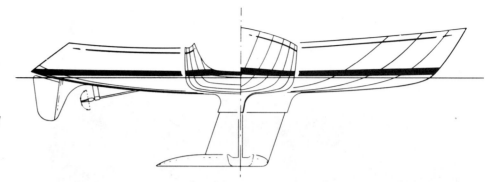

Figure 9-4

Lines of a 57-foot performance motorsailer, **Quicksilver,** *designed by the author to achieve 14 knots under both sail and power. She is powered by a 275-horsepower diesel driving a 38-inch geared folding propeller at 750 RPM.*

gives the maximum area is nearly rectangular. Such a shape also places more of the blade area at the tips, where it can do the most work. It is the opinion of the author that a wide, rectangular-contour-bladed, geared folding propeller of large diameter will give the best combination of speed under power and low drag under sail. The key is to use a very large reduction gear so that the propeller can be of the largest possible diameter. Such a propeller can give very impressive performance.

Figure 9-4 shows the lines (including propeller, shaft and strut arrangement) of a 57-foot sailboat designed by the author to do 14 knots under sail and 14 knots under power. She is fitted with a 38-inch-diameter geared folding propeller, driven by a 275 HP diesel.

Figure 9-5

Time-lapse photo of a typical geared folding two-bladed propeller. Note the wide, square-contour blades and the extremely low-drag shape when folded.

(Courtesy of Jastram Ltd.)

Shaft speed is only 750 RPM. With any other type of propeller, top sailing speed would have been severely limited as a result of the additional drag from the greater exposed blade area.

Controllable-Pitch Propellers for Motorsailers

At the other end of the spectrum are large, heavy-displacement motorsailers, which can be expected to operate under both sail and power a great deal of the time. This presents them with many of the same variable-loading problems experienced by tugs and trawlers (see Chapter 8). For such craft, fully-feathering, controllable-pitch propellers are the best solution. All controllable-pitch propellers are more expensive, but the increase in control and performance is well worth the cost. When fully feathered, these propellers have no more drag than normal fully feathering propellers. The ability to adjust pitch at will while underway, though, permits maximum thrust at minimum engine RPM and HP in all possible conditions.

Using the Slip Method to Calculate a Sailboat Propeller

For most sailboats, the slip method is adequate for selecting a propeller. The calculation may be made as usual for a standard three-bladed fixed propeller with a MWR of 0.33. The adjustment factors from Table 5-2 for two-bladed propellers should be used as required. Table 6-3 should then be consulted to adjust efficiency for the reduced area of the narrower blades, if applicable. Finally, since the propeller will be folding or feathering, the efficiency should be reduced to 90 or 95 percent, respectively, of the values found from these tables. (A poor propeller design can give even lower efficiencies.)

Some Auxiliaries Accept Small Amounts of Cavitation

Blade loading should be checked as described in Chapter 5. Note, though, that many sailboat propeller installations accept the vibration and loss of thrust from high blade loading in order to use narrow blades and limit drag under sail. Since most sailing auxiliaries power only a few dozen hours out of the year, the additional wear and tear of cavitation can be an acceptable compromise. For larger motorsailers, and all long-distance cruisers that will power over 30 percent of the time, adjustments to propeller diameter and blade width should be made to eliminate cavitation as described in Chapter 5. If no detailed information is available on the developed blade area—as is often the case with sailboat propellers—a mean width ratio of 0.21 and a disc area ratio of 0.24 can be used as a good general starting point.

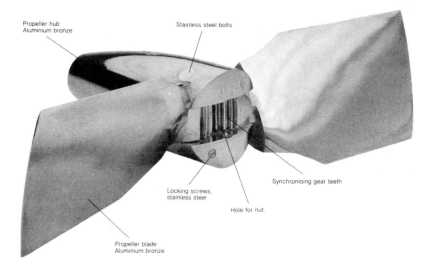

Figure 9-6

A stern view of the same geared folding propeller shown in Figure 9-5.

(Courtesy of Jastram Ltd.)

Using the Bp-δ Method to Calculate a Sailboat Propeller

For heavier motorsailers, the Bp-δ method should be used. The difficulty with applying the Bp-δ method to calculating propellers for sailboats is that wake factor estimates are problematical. The additional drag and resistance from their large keels make the values from Wake Factor vs Block Coefficient Chart 6-1 or Formula 6-1 unreliable. Instead, wake factors for sailboats should be estimated as in Table 9-1:

Table 9-1

TABLE 9-1   SAILBOAT WAKE FACTORS (Wf)

Propeller Location	Wake Factor
In badly-faired aperture	0.80
In well-faired aperture	0.85
In the open on a centerline strut	0.89
In the open on a strut offset from the centerline	0.91

The values in the table are necessarily estimates. As a consequence, the Bp-δ method will not always give more reliable results than the slip method for sailboats. It does, however, give better understanding of the variables in selecting the propeller for each design. As with the slip method, the propeller calculation should be made based on a standard three-bladed fixed propeller and adjustments from Table 5-2 and Table 6-3 should be used as appropriate. Assume that efficiencies for folding propellers are 90 percent of the values found in this way, and for feathering propellers, 95 percent. Finally, blade loading should be checked and adjustments to eliminate cavitation made, again as described in Chapter 5.

OUTBOARDS AND GO-FAST WRINKLES

Outboard Propeller Selection

Propellers for outboards are determined in exactly the same way as for other vessels. In most instances, the information available about boat speed, engine performance and propeller shape does not justify using the Bp-δ method, and the slip method will give adequate results. As with all other propellers, the actual shaft horsepower and the actual RPM at the propeller after the reduction gear are the critical factors—along with boat speed. Most outboard manufacturers (unlike inboard manufacturers) now rate engine horsepower at the shaft, so no further deductions need to be made.

Outboard Shaft Speed and Lower-Unit Gearing

Shaft speed is determined by the reduction gear in the lower unit. Consult the manufacturer as to the reduction gears available. For low speed workboats and sailboats, many manufacturers offer heavy-duty and/or sailor models, with large reduction ratios. For ordinary runabouts, planing power cruisers, and ski boats, standard models will have suitable reduction gears, while all-out racers can obtain custom gears, with low ratios for higher shaft speed, from manufacturers specializing in high-speed outboard power.

Further, heavy, low-speed outboard craft often can benefit from four- and even five-bladed propellers to overcome the limitations in diameter caused by the size and shape of the lower unit and the location of the cavitation plate.

Figure 9-7

A typical outboard-motor propeller. Note that most standard outboards vent their exhaust through the propeller hub. The three slots or holes in the hub are for this purpose. This is a convenient system, but it decreases useful blade area by increasing hub diameter. Such hubs are around 30 percent of diameter as opposed to around 20 percent for standard propellers. Some performance-oriented outboards avoid this problem by venting exhaust above the propeller.

(Courtesy of The Michigan Wheel Company)

Figure 9-8

A typical performance-outboard or stern-drive propeller. The smaller hub diameter allowed by not venting exhaust through the hub permits greater blade area and more efficient blade shape in the same diameter propeller.

(Courtesy of The Michigan Wheel Company)

"Jacking" or Lifting an Outboard

On most average runabouts and cruisers, the outboard is positioned so that the cavitation plate—just above the propeller—is about 1 inch (25 mm) below the bottom of the hull. As boat speed increases, the drag of the lower unit becomes an important factor. Accordingly, on high-speed craft—boats operating consistently over 35 knots—the outboard is lifted vertically. This is called "jacking up the motor" and reduces appendage drag at high speed simply by lifting some of the appendage out of the water. The most sophisticated high-speed craft are fitted with hydraulic jacking plates that allow fingertip raising and lowering of the engine while underway.

Like all such adjustments, jacking has its limits. If the propeller is lifted too far, it will begin to suck air down from the surface, causing ventilation. (This is frequently and mistakenly called cavitation, which is quite different—see Chapter 4.) Blades that are raked aft help delay the onset of ventilation somewhat. A jacked-up propeller also delivers somewhat less thrust than its deeper counterpart, since it works in the slightly less dense and more turbulent water near the surface. Another factor is that when a propeller is deep in the water, it tends to push the bow up slightly (the propeller's thrust line projects well below the boat's center of gravity—see Chapter 7). Both the additional thrust of the deep propeller and its tendency to lift the bow assist in breaking out onto a plane. Conversely, a well jacked-up propeller near the surface is less efficient at breaking a boat out onto a plane, although it is a faster configuration once high speed is attained.

Outboard Tilt or Trim

The tilt or trim of an outboard is critical to planing performance. Trimming the motor out—that is, with the lower unit and propeller away from the hull—tilts the thrust line down. This pushes the stern down and lifts the bow. Conversely, trimming the motor in—lower unit towards the hull—tilts the thrust line up, lifting the transom and depressing the bow. Generally, out trim helps a boat break onto a plane more easily. As planing speed is achieved, somewhat less out trim should be used.

In theory, the greater the planing angle, the more the lift and the better the planing performance. In practice, excessive planing angle causes the hull underbody to have too large an angle of attack, and the hull "stalls." Most conventional vee-bottom hulls operate best at about a 4 to 5 degree planing angle. In addition, large amounts of out trim depress the transom enough to actually place an additional load on the hull, exactly as if the boat had been made heavier. Obviously, this makes a boat slower. Hydraulic power trim is the answer. Like hydraulic jacking plates, hydraulic power trim allows the operator to achieve optimum trim angle while underway.

Mounting Outboards on Transom Brackets

Another speed refinement on performance-oriented craft is to mount the outboard on brackets that support it well aft of the transom—usually 18 to 24 inches. There are several advantages to transom brackets. First, they shift the weight of the engine aft, helping to lift the bow. Second, they move the propeller further away from the shadow of the hull, allowing it to get slightly freer water inflow. Third, shifting the engine weight aft permits lifting or jacking the engine somewhat more than is possible immediately behind the boat. This is partly because the engine weight aft helps counteract the loss of bow-up thrust from not having a deep propeller, and partly because the water aft of the hull rises slightly as it flows aft.

Transom brackets have the further practical advantage on all craft of freeing up more interior room, since the forward face of the outboard no longer projects into the vessel through the transom well.

INBOARD/OUTBOARDS OR STERN DRIVES

The preceding comments regarding outboards apply to sterndrives, outdrives or inboard/outboards, with the exception, of course, of motor-jacking and bracket-mounting.

Most standard stern drives are similar to outboard lower units; however, industrial-grade sterndrives, which can fit proportionately larger propellers and may even be made of solid bronze, rather than the usual cast aluminum, are available. The advantages of outdrives for larger, heavy craft are the added maneuverability gained from being able to steer them like an outboard, and increased freedom to operate in shallow water due to their ability to kick up on striking bottom.

SURFACE PROPELLERS

Surface propellers are the ultimate combination of the beneficial effects of motor-jacking, and the advantages of a steerable sterndrive. Surface propellers are designed to work half in and half out of the water. They are mounted on the transom aft—like a stern drive—but are configured so that their shaft centerline falls only just below the water surface at rest.

These propellers only come into their own at speeds of over 35 knots, and are really justified at speeds of over 40 knots. In such conditions the surface drive, being largely out of the water, offers the least appendage drag possible, while at the same time avoiding cavitation by having the blades fully aerated all the time. Of course, with ordinary propellers, aeration or ventilation is undesirable, but surface propellers are specifically designed to operate in this way. Among other things, surface propellers are usually about 30 to 40 percent larger in diameter than comparable standard propellers.

If high speed, maneuverability, and shoal draft are prime considerations, a surface propeller is an excellent, although expensive, solution. The reduction of appendage drag can increase speed by 10 to 12 percent. (On a 50-knot craft, this would be an increase of about 6.5 knots, to about 56.5 knots.) Sizing of a surface propeller cannot be done in the usual way, so the manufacturer must be consulted in the selection.

CONTRA-ROTATING PROPELLERS

When a propeller accelerates water into itself from ahead and expels it astern, it generates thrust, exactly like a jet engine. Unfortunately, a sizeable percentage of the power delivered to the propeller also goes into twisting the water around, creating the helically

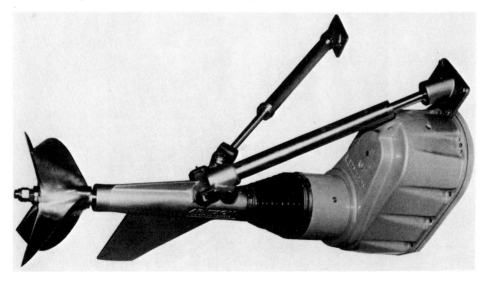

Figure 9-9

A typical surface drive unit. This unit steers like an outboard or conventional stern drive via the hydraulic ram on the side. The hydraulic ram on the top allows adjustment of vertical trim, effectively giving the operator a propeller of variable diameter.

(Courtesy of Arneson Marine, Inc.)

Figure 9-10

A racing catamaran powered with twin surface drives. Such extremely high-speed craft gain the most from a surface drive installation.

(Courtesy of Arneson Marine, Inc.)

shaped propeller wake. This rotational energy is doing nothing to drive the boat—it is just waste.

Contra-rotating propellers eliminate this waste. In this type of installation, two propellers are positioned one immediately ahead of the other on the same shaft line, but rotating in opposite directions. The rotational energy imparted to the water by the forward propeller is cancelled out by the opposite rotation of the aft propeller. The slipstream from contra-rotating propellers is nearly smooth and straight, with little twist. Such propellers are, in theory, between 5 and 20 percent more efficient than standard single propellers, but 8 to 10 percent is a realistic practical range.

Figure 9-11

A steerable Z-drive unit with contra-rotating propellers.

(Courtesy of Aquamaster-Ruma Ltd.)

The most common configuration for contra-rotating propellers involves a propeller of smaller diameter and more blades behind a propeller of larger diameter and fewer blades. This is because the astern propeller is working in a faster water flow than the ahead propeller, and as a result, it must have a smaller diameter and steeper pitch. At the same time, both propellers should be absorbing the same horsepower—hence the additional blade on the after propeller.

Because of the large number of blades—usually seven or nine, in total—a contra-rotating propeller system has more blade area and thus lower blade loading than a comparable single propeller at the same horsepower. This reduces cavitation problems, and the large number of blades greatly diminishes vibration.

The drawback to contra-rotating propellers is their tremendous complexity. Not only does this increase the cost of contra-rotating propellers to far above that of comparable standard single propellers, but it also increases the level of maintenance required. Further, some of the gain in efficiency from thrust is lost to additional frictional resistance in the many extra gears and bearings. Nevertheless, contra-rotating propellers can offer some actual gains in operating efficiency.

Volvo puts out high-power sterndrives equipped with contra-rotating propellers (three-bladed forward and four-bladed aft), and Aquamaster is offering a steerable Z-drive unit (see Chapter 8) with contra-rotating propellers (four-bladed forward and five-bladed aft) for commercial applications. Most boats report only modest increases in speed with the Volvo units, but noticeably improved handling and smoothness of operation. The Aquamaster unit is not intended to increase speed, but rather to increase thrust and efficiency for fuel savings. An efficiency increase of about 9 percent is expected.

Appendix A
Measuring the Hull
Procedure for Determining Displacement

In Chapter 2 we discussed the importance of knowing exactly how much a boat weighs when making speed and powering estimates. In later chapters, we found that we had to know the block coefficient, waterline beam and draft of the hull body. If this information is not available from the original builder or designer, you must measure the hull itself.

Measuring a hull for this purpose is not difficult, and seldom requires more than an afternoon of work to get the actual measurements; however, it must be done with care and patience. The procedure outlined below is actually identical to taking off the lines of a boat. For the purpose of simply estimating displacement, though, far fewer points have to be measured, and the acceptable level of accuracy is somewhat lower.

Measuring the boat or "taking off" can be divided into three basic steps.

1. Leveling the boat and establishing a reference line for measurements.
2. Measurement of three critical stations.
3. Transferring this information to paper and using the result to find displacement.

It will help if you can find an assistant to help with positioning and recording measurements during the taking off process.

ESTABLISHING BASE DIMENSIONS

Mark the Waterline Afloat

With the vessel afloat in calm water, carefully mark the waterline, at rest in the normal, fully-loaded condition (two-thirds fuel, water, and cargo, and full crew and equipment). Marks should be made at the stem face, and the aftermost point of the waterline, as well as at midships. Additional intermediate marks can be helpful.

Haul the Boat and Level Athwartships and Fore-and-Aft

The boat should then be hauled and leveled fore-and-aft and athwartships. Leave space to work around the hull on at least one side. To determine level, attach a plumb bob to the waterline at the bow and stern. Carefully draw a dark, contrasting vertical line down the center of the stem or keel face. Use wedges, shims and jacks to adjust athwartships trim until—sighting aft, from forward—the bow plumb bob lines up with the vertical line.

Next, adjust fore-and-aft trim until the length of the fore and after plumb bobs to the ground is identical. It is often not possible to truly level the boat fore and aft because the entire boatyard may have a pronounced slope, but as long as the sloped surface is smooth and flat, this will not present a problem. If the yard surface is uneven and bumpy, the reference line must be set to match the fore-and-aft angle of the waterline, and subsequent measurements must be taken at right angles to it.

Setting up the Reference Line and Determining Waterline Length

Now measure the length between the plumb bobs and set up a reference line. To do this, we'll need two long, straight boards (our transverse boards) about 80 to 90 percent as long as the beam of the boat. Draw a straight line—the transverse line—down the center of each board. Make a cross or reference point a few inches from one end and mark it "boat centerline." Then measure out along each transverse line exactly the same distance (about 75 percent of beam) and make a tick mark on each labeled "reference-line centerline." Set heavy nails or spikes vertically through the two reference-line centerline tick marks. Place the transverse boards at the bow and stern of the vessel so they project out at right angles from the boat centerline with the plumb bobs centered over the boat centerline crossmarks. Use a carpenter's level along with shims and wedges to adjust the transverse boards to level.

Stretch a reference line taut between the two spikes, resting it just on top of the transverse boards. Adjust the angles of the transverse boards, and the length of the reference line, so that they cross each other at exactly right angles (a large carpenter's square will be adequate for this), making sure that the boat centerline cross marks remain centered under the fore-and-aft plumb bobs. When all is square, fix the transverse boards firmly in place with heavy weights and or spikes. The squared-up transverse boards and the taut reference line will form the reference points for all subsequent hull measurements (see Figure A-1).

Measuring along the reference line from spike to spike yields the exact waterline length of the vessel. Make marks on the reference line at one-half, one-quarter, and three-quarters of the waterline length (stations 0.50, 0.25, and 0.75). These points establish the fore-and-aft location of the midship station and the stations at 25 percent and 75 percent of the waterline. Measuring these three stations will provide sufficient information to estimate displacement.

MEASURING THREE CRITICAL SECTIONS

Making a Triangulation Frame from Scrap Lumber

There are a number of methods for measuring section shape. One of the easiest and most reliable is to make a triangulation frame out of scrap plywood. The base board of the

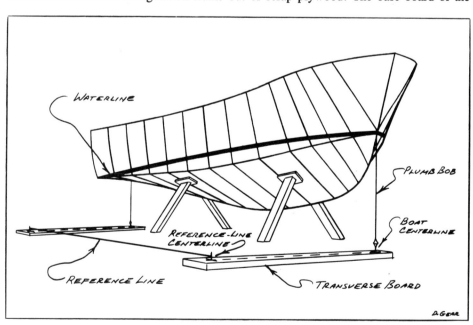

Figure A-1

Establishing base dimensions.

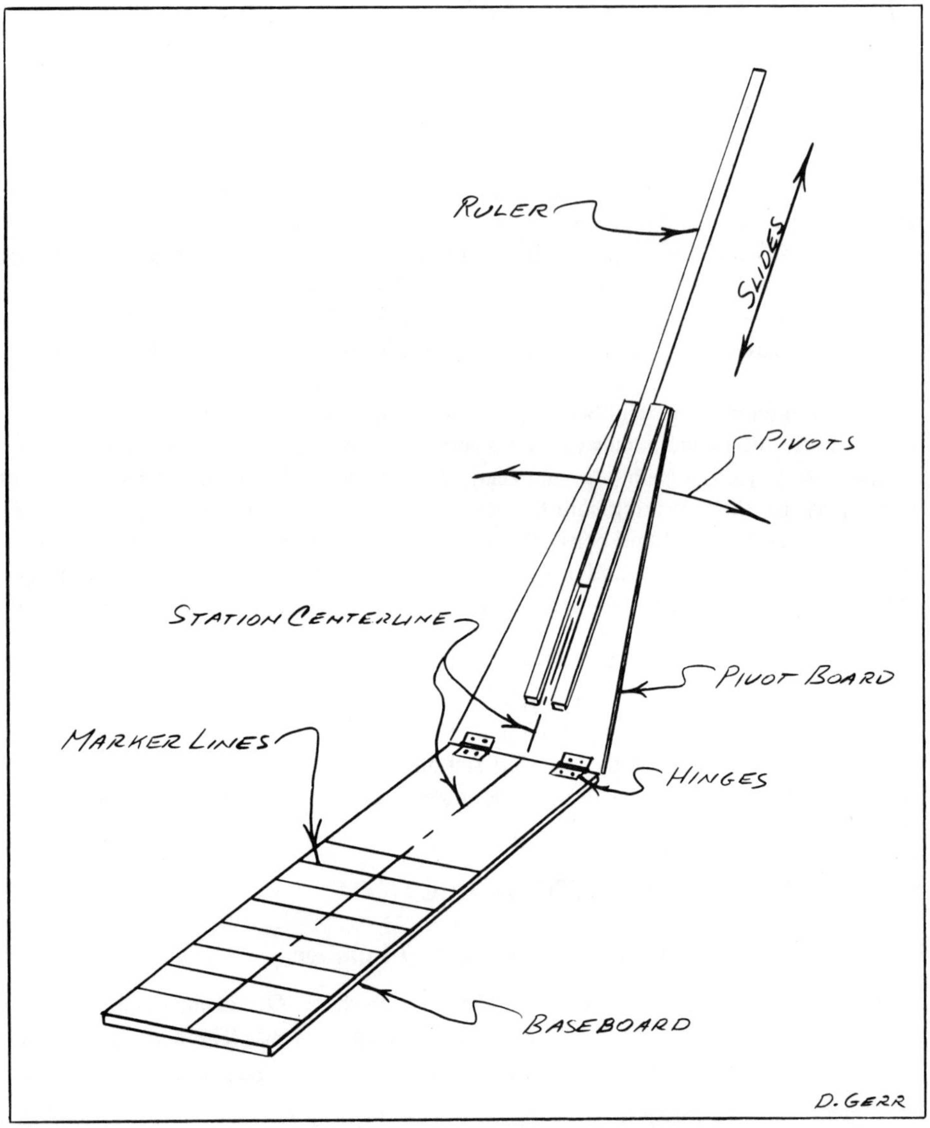

Figure A-2

Triangulation frame.

frame should be made of ½-inch (12 mm) plywood about one-half of the beam of the boat long, and two to three feet wide. Cut a roughly triangular piece of ½-inch plywood (the pivot board) about one-third the beam of the boat long and attach it to the end of the base with two hinges so that it can swing up at any angle, but not shift from side to side. On top of the pivot board, hammer a set of frames or guides together to accept a standard 2-inch (50 mm) wide aluminum ruler. The ruler should be free to slide in the guides but have as little play as possible. Set the guides so that the ruler projects at exactly right angles to the pivot-board hinge axis. Aluminum rulers are quite inexpensive, and are available in a wide variety of lengths. You will probably need two, one about 50 percent of beam, and one about 25 percent of beam in length (see Figure A-2).

Draw a "station centerline" along the length of the baseboard and pivot board. On the baseboard, draw a series of regularly-spaced marker lines (say, three inches apart) crossing the station centerline at exactly right angles. Measure and mark the distances along the station centerline of the baseboard from each marker line to the hinge axis. On the pivot board, measure the distance along the station centerline from the hinge axis to the opposite edge of the pivot board, and record this distance on the pivot board. Finally, install the ruler guides, placing them so that one edge of the ruler runs exactly along the station centerline. We are now ready to measure the midships section.

Taking the Station Measurements with the Triangulation Frame

Place the triangulation frame at the midships station so that the baseboard lies flat on the ground under the reference line, with the pivot board end facing the hull. Make sure that the station centerline crosses the reference line at right angles, precisely at the midship-station mark made earlier on the reference line. This is simply done by lining up one of the baseboard marker lines so that it is exactly parallel and directly beneath the reference line. Raise up the baseboard so that it just touches the reference line. Measuring with a level, shim the baseboard so that it is horizontal in the boat's athwartship plane. Record the baseboard's marker line position carefully—you will be using this position for a whole series of measurements.

Hold the triangulation frame firmly in place with heavy weights. Then, insert the most conveniently sized ruler into the pivot board guides and lift the pivot board, sliding the ruler out until it just touches the hull at the waterline. Mark this point on the hull with a grease pencil, as point 1, and record the length of the ruler projecting beyond the edge of the pivot board. (It is not necessary to measure the angle of the pivot board, as we will see shortly.)

Repeat this process at 6- to 18-inch (150 - 450 mm) intervals down the side of the hull, marking each point on the hull and assigning it a number with the grease pencil, and recording the ruler length and baseboard reference marker line for that point. On most hulls, 10 to 15 points should be measured for each station. Simple, single-chine hulls can be measured with fewer points, while complex, wineglass-section hulls require more. Be sure to take a number of measurements on and close to all changes in hull shape, for instance, at the garboard (where the hull meets the keel), at the bottom of the keel and at the turn of the bilge or chine. It may be necessary to move the baseboard to a new marker line—sliding it in towards the hull—to get measurements close to the keel.

When you have measured as many points as desirable with the baseboard set at one marker line, slide the baseboard into a new marker line position, but still at the same midships station. Relevel the triangulation frame, record the new marker line position, and then carefully measure each marked point on the hull again, recording the ruler lengths to the pivot board as before. In this way, since every point is measured twice, each point is triangulated and defined very exactly.

When you have finished with the midships section, use the same procedure for the stations at 25 percent and 75 percent of the waterline. Once you've completed these measurements, the taking off job is finished. It only remains to make sense out of the data.

FINDING DISPLACEMENT FROM THE MEASUREMENTS

Drawing the Three Measured Sections to Scale

You can now take a sheet of paper and draw the hull sections you have measured to any convenient scale. (It is well worth spending the few dollars it costs to buy an architect's six-sided scale rule for this purpose.)

Draw a horizontal line representing the ground, or baseline, and a vertical line representing the boat centerline. Choose a convenient scale—say one-half inch equals one foot—and measure the distance out from the boat centerline to the reference-line centerline on the transverse boards. Mark this point on the baseline. Now measure in from the reference line the distance from each of the marker line settings you actually used to the pivot point on the triangulation frame, and mark each on the baseline. (If, for instance, you used marker lines 2, 4 and 8, mark these points as such on your drawing.)

To locate the first hull point, add the distance the ruler projects beyond the pivot board to the length of the pivot board and set a standard draftsman's compass to that distance in the scale you are using. Set the point of the dividers on the appropriate marker-line mark and draw a light pencil-line arc. Repeat this process for the same point, say point 1 at the waterline, but now using the second baseboard marker-line position. You will now have two arcs that cross at the point you measured on the hull.

Repeat this procedure for each point you measured at the station, and soon you will have defined each point along the hull, but now on paper, in scale. Repeat this process for the other two stations. Then draw a horizontal line (parallel to the baseline) through the highest (waterline) point at each station, and connect the other points in a smooth curve. This gives the shape of each station you have measured.

Using your architect's scale, you can now measure the beam at the waterline directly from the midships-station half section. (Remember that since you've only drawn half a station, you'll have to multiply by two to get full beam at the waterline.) To determine depth of hull, measure from the waterline to the intersection of the keel; for extreme draft, measure to the bottom of the keel. (If the draft is greatest at the stern, you can set the triangulation frame aft and take a series of measurements there to find maximum draft.)

Finding the Areas of Each Measured Section

What remains now is to find the areas of each of these sections and use that information to find the volume and thus the displacement of the hull. Naval architects use an instrument called a planimeter for this purpose. Without this expensive tool, the easiest way to procede is to purchase transparent graph paper of convenient scale and lay it on top of your half sections. (If the sections are drawn to the one-half-inch-equals-one-foot scale [1:24], and the graph paper is divided into inches with each inch subdivided into tenths, then each small square on the graph paper will equal 0.04 square feet of area [37.16 cm²].)

To calculate the area, simply count all the squares contained in each of the sections. You'll need to do some estimating—if a square falls about one-third in and two-thirds

Figure A-3

Drawing the measured section.

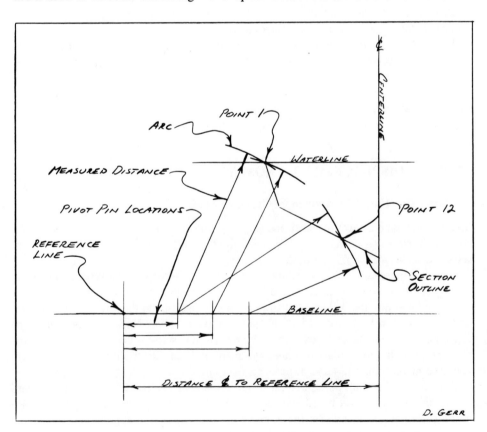

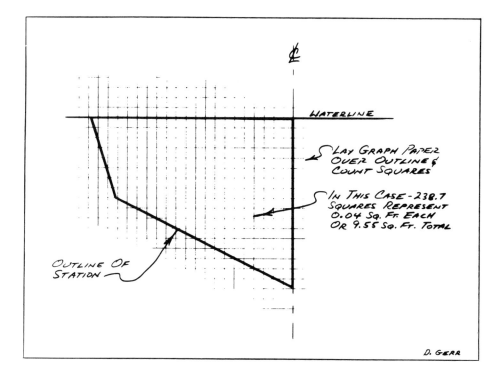

Figure A-4

Measuring section area.

out of the section, count it as one-third of a square. If the midships station, for example, contains 238 of the 0.04 square foot (37.16 cm²) squares, then the station half-area would be 9.55 square feet (0.88 m²), and the full section area would be twice that, or 19.1 square feet (1.76 m²).

Finding Hull Volume From Station Area

To find the hull volume in cubic feet, add the three full section areas and multiply by the distance between stations. If the waterline is 40 feet (12.2 m), and the three stations we measured are spaced at one-quarter of this distance, the space between them is 10 feet (3.05 m). Now, if the station at 25 percent of the waterline aft of the bow had a full-section area of 8.9 square feet (0.83 m²), and the station at 75 percent of the waterline length aft of the bow had a full-section area of 14.2 square feet (1.32 m²), we would find hull volume as follows:

Station	Full Section Area
0.25	8.9
0.50	19.1
0.75	14.2

Total Areas = 42.2 square feet

42.2 square feet × 10 foot station spacing = 422 cubic feet (11.95 m³)

422 cubic feet × 64 pound/cubic foot (weight of sea water) = 27,000 pounds or 12 long tons (12247 kg, or 12.2 metric tons).

If care has been taken with the measurements and with the drawing of the three sections, the displacement found by this method will be accurate to within about 4 or 5 percent. This displacement figure can now be used in the speed and powering formulas, the block-coefficient formula, the displacement-length-ratio formula, and so on, for reliable propeller calculations.

FINDING QUARTER-BEAM BUTTOCK ANGLE

The quarter-beam-buttock angle may be found from the midships section and the section at 75 percent of the waterline aft of the bow. Measure half of the half-beam (the quarter beam) out from the boat centerline on the baseline, and draw a vertical line from this point on the baseline up through the half sections. Measure the height above the baseline at which the quarter beam buttock line intersects the underside of the midships station and the station at 75 percent.

On a separate sheet, draw a long baseline and make two tick marks on it, spaced exactly the distance of the station spacing in the scale chosen. (In our example, this is at 10 feet (3.05 m), in the 1:24 scale.) Draw two vertical lines through these tick marks and mark, on the right-hand vertical, the height above the base of the quarter-beam buttock at midships and, on the left-hand vertical, the height of the quarter-beam buttock at the station at 75 percent. Draw a straight line between these two points and measure the angle it makes with the baseline. This is the quarter-beam buttock angle. (See Chapter 2.)

Appendix B
Measuring the Propeller
Procedure for Finding Diameter and Pitch

It's frequently useful to be able to measure a propeller's diameter, pitch and blade area. This way you can check an existing propeller for suitability, ensure that twin-screw vessels are actually fitted with propellers of identical dimensions, or determine if a new propeller really corresponds to the measurements specified.

MEASURING DIAMETER

Finding the diameter is quite straightforward. Measure the radius of the propeller from the shaft centerline out to the tip of one blade. Obviously, the radius doubled gives the diameter.

MEASURING BLADE AREA

Making a Paper Template

Measuring expanded blade area is nearly as direct. Take ordinary paper (brown wrapping paper works well) and temporarily glue it (use paper cement) flat and flush along the surface of one blade. Carefully trim the paper with a pair of scissors or a knife to match the outline of the blade, and peel it off. Except for minor differences caused by blade-surface convexity, this paper template will be an exact reproduction of the expanded blade shape and area.

Finding Template Area with the Trapezoidal Rule

To find the expanded area, we use the trapezoidal rule. Lay the blade template flat and draw a straight line along its center (the blade centerline), from the root to the tip. Divide the centerline into ten equal segments—using eleven cross lines, with cross line "0" exactly at the blade root and cross line "10" exactly at the blade tip. The cross lines must meet the blade centerline at right angles. Measure the distance between the segment lines and the length of each segment. Add the segment lengths, using one-half of the lengths for segments "0" and "10," and multiply by the distance between segments. The answer is the expanded blade area.

For example if the blade segments are spaced at 1.45 inches (36.8 mm) and the segment lengths measure as follows, we find:

Cross Lines	Cross Line Lengths		Trapezoidal Rule Lengths
0	1.68″	divided by 2 =	0.84″
1	3.38″		3.38″
2	5.56″		5.56″
3	6.58″		6.58″
4	7.12″		7.12″
5	7.36″		7.36″
6	7.29″		7.29″
7	6.95″		6.95″
8	6.34″		6.34″
9	5.10″		5.10″
10	0.00″	divided by 2 =	0.00″
		Total =	56.52″

Taking this total, we work out the area as follows: **[56.52 inches × 1.45 inch cross-line spacing = 81.9 square inch blade area (528.4 cm²).]** Multiplying by the number of blades gives the total expanded area. If this were a four-bladed propeller, for example, the total area would be 327.6 square inches (2113.5 cm²).

Determining Hub Diameter and Blade-Area Ratios

You can take maximum blade width directly from the above table of measured segments; in this case it will be 7.36 inches (187 mm) at cross line 5. Blade length from root to tip is simply measured along the blade centerline—14.5 inches (367 mm) in our example.

Figure B-1

Measuring propeller pitch with a right triangle.

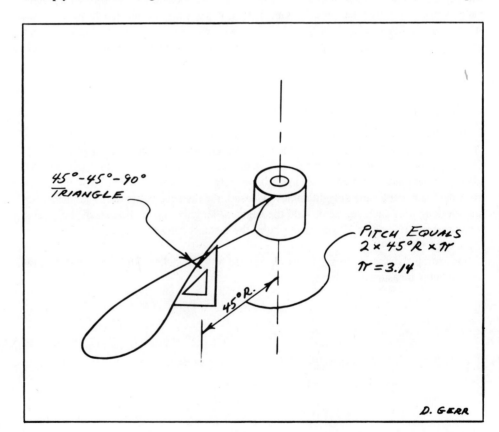

Find the hub diameter by subtracting two times the blade length (from root to tip) from the overall diameter. If overall diameter is 34.8 inches (884 mm), then hub diameter would be 5.8 inches (147 mm). Using all this information in the blade area and blade area ratio formulas in Chapter 4, we can determine disc area, disc-area ratio, mean-width ratio and so on.

MEASURING PITCH

Finding Radius for Pitch at 45 Degrees

Establishing pitch is more difficult. Without special measuring tools, you'll have to pull the propeller and lay it face up, on a smooth, flat surface. Holding a 45-degree right triangle (45° -45° - 90 °) at right angles to the propeller's radius line, slide it along the length of the blade—between the blade backs and the ground—until it just fits beneath the contour of the blade. Measure the distance from the centerline, and you have found the radius at which the propeller pitch is 45 degrees. The true pitch is two times this radius times π (≈3.14). You will have to make some allowance, by eye, for any convexity of the blade backs.

If at 6.5 inches (165 mm) from the centerline our example propeller has a pitch of 45 degrees its true pitch would be 40.8 inches (1036 mm) **[6.5 in. 45° pitch radius × 2 × 3.14 = 40.8 inches].** With our measured diameter of 34.8 inches (884 mm), this gives a pitch ratio of 1.17.

Advantages of a Pitchometer

The difficulty with the foregoing method is that the propeller must be taken off the shaft. Even on quite small craft this can be a time-consuming task. On larger vessels, the labor involved is often prohibitive. The solution is to use a pitchometer—an instrument specially designed to measure propeller pitch. Although these instruments cost at least two to three hundred dollars, this is usually far less than the cost of hauling a boat, pulling the propeller, and reinstalling it. A good pitchometer will enable you to measure pitch with the boat still in the water.

Jack Laird, an engineer with Caterpillar Inc. and with his own consulting firm, Laird Engineering, has perfected a patented pitchometer that meets all the above requirements. Figure B-2 shows his compact pitchometer from both sides, and B-3 describes its use. Those interested in obtaining Laird's pitchometer should contact him at either Caterpillar Inc., or Laird Engineering (see list of manufacturers and suppliers on p. 000).

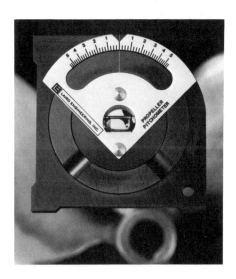 

Figure B-2

Front and back views of Jack Laird's pitchometer.

(Courtesy of Jack Laird and Caterpillar, Inc.)

INTRODUCTION

The 8T5322 Pitchometer is now available for use in measuring the pitch (angle) of the blades on a marine engine propeller. The 8T5322 Pitchometer provides a much simpler and faster method of checking blade pitch, and gives the same accuracy of an equivalent fixed installation propeller pitch checking system.

FEATURES

The 8T5322 Pitchometer provides a method of measuring blade pitch, at any point on the blade, as follows:

a) Without removal of the propeller from the propeller shaft.

b) At any angle.

c) In any position, including underwater, if necessary.

Some further advantages of the 8T5322 Pitchometer are:

d) Makes it possible to check/measure propeller pitch when the propeller is stored in the horizontal position and/or before the propeller is installed on the propeller shaft.

e) Aids in determining which blades need to be "re-pitched", and by how much.

f) Helps in reducing propeller vibration by giving an accurate check to ensure that all blades are at the same pitch.

g) Gives improved efficiency by ensuring the correct pitch for the propeller blades of all propellers on a multi-propeller installation.

PITCHOMETER ACCURACY: ± 2%

8T5322 PITCHOMETER NOMENCLATURE

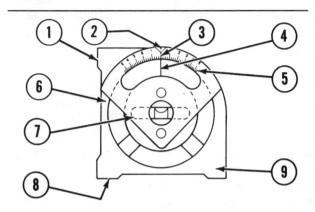

1. Vertical Edge.
2. Housing Index Mark.
3. Scale Index Mark.
4. Compensating Ring Index Mark.
5. Scale.
6. Compensating Ring.
7. Scale/Level Vial Holder.
8. Horizontal Edge.
9. Housing.

PROPELLER PITCH CHECK
(Propeller Installed on Shaft)

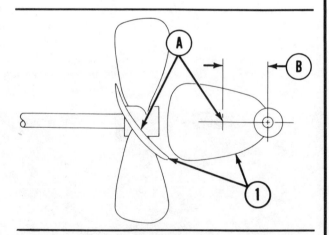

1. On propeller blade ① that is to be checked, make a mark Ⓐ on the rear face of the blade.

2. Measure and record distance Ⓑ (from mark Ⓐ to the center of the propeller shaft).

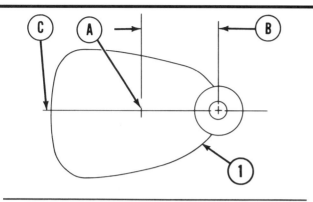

3. Locate and mark centerline Ⓒ through mark Ⓐ on the blade.

4. Turn propeller blade ① so it is in a horizontal position.

5. Turn compensating ring ② and scale/level vial holder ③ so scale index mark Ⓓ and compensating ring index mark Ⓔ are in alignment with housing index mark Ⓕ. (This is the starting position when using the pitchometer.)

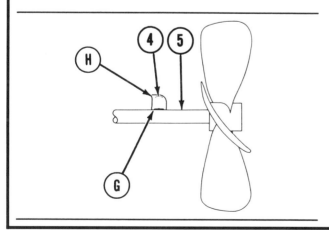

6. With pitchometer ④ components positioned as indicated in Step 5, put pitchometer ④ on propeller shaft ⑤ as shown. [Horizontal edge Ⓖ on shaft ⑤ and vertical edge Ⓗ to face toward engine.]

7. To compensate for shaft angle, turn compensating ring ② and scale/vial level holder ③ so the bubble in the level is centered (indicates level condition). (Hold compensating ring ② and scale/vial level holder in this position. Do not permit them to move.)

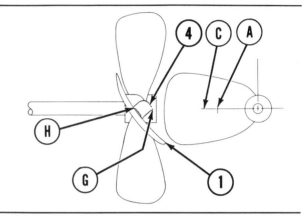

8. Put pitchometer ④ on blade ① so vertical edge Ⓗ is on mark Ⓐ. Position pitchometer ④ so it is centered over centerline Ⓒ.

9. Hold compensating ring ② firmly, (it must not move) while turning scale/level vial holder ③ to center (level) the bubble in the vial.

10. Record the scale reading at compensating ring index mark Ⓔ.

11. Multiply the value recorded in Step 10 by the measurement recorded as dimension Ⓑ (see Steps 1 and 2). (This is the distance from the centerline of propeller shaft to the center of mark Ⓐ on the propeller blade.) The product of this exercise is the amount of blade pitch at mark Ⓐ.

EXAMPLE:
Dimension Ⓑ = 20.0"
Scale Reading = 2.25"
20.0" × 2.25" = 45" pitch

12. Do Steps 1–11 at enough points on each propeller blade, to be sure that propeller pitch is the same over the full area of a blade, and that all blades have the same pitch.

Figure B-3   How to use the pitchometer, as described in a Caterpillar pamphlet.

Appendix C
Shaft Taper and Coupling Dimensions

The following recommendations for the dimensions and configurations of propeller-shaft couplings, hubs, and endings are taken from Society of Automotive Engineers standards, as set forth in their publications SAE J756 and SAE J755. For more information contact the SAE, 400 Commonwealth Drive, Warrendale, Pennsylvania 15096.

1. <u>SCOPE</u>: This SAE Standard covers propeller shaft couplings for use with propeller shafts up to 3 inches outside diameter.

2. <u>PURPOSE</u>: To provide design guidance that results in dimensional interchangeability of marine propeller-shaft couplings within the scope of this standard.

3. <u>GENERAL</u>: Includes couplings with an internal pilot diameter (Type I) with tapered or straight bores, and external pilot diameter (Type II) couplings with straight bores.

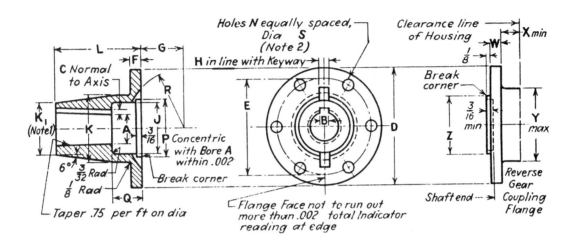

FIG. 1--TYPE I PROPELLER-SHAFT COUPLING, INTERNAL PILOT, TAPER BORE,
SAE FLANGE NOS. 1, 2, 3, AND 4

Note 1--Hub outside taper is optional.
Note 2--No. 1 flange coupling bolt is to be 3/8--24 X 1-1/4 with plain nut and
lockwasher.
No. 2 flange coupling bolt is to be 7/16--20 X 1-1/2 with plain nut and
lockwasher.
No. 3 flange coupling bolt is to be 1/2--20 X 1-3/4 with plain nut and
lockwasher.
No. 4 flange coupling bolt is to be 5/8--18 X 2 with plain nut and
lockwasher.
Note 3--See Table 4 for taper bore dimensions A, B, and C.
Note 4--All dimensions are in inches unless otherwise stated (1 in = 25.4 mm;
1 ft = 304.8 mm).

TABLE 1
PROPELLER-SHAFT COUPLINGS, TYPE I, INTERNAL PILOT--TAPER BORE[a]

SAE Flange No.	Shaft Dia Max	D	E	F	G	H	J	K	K_1	L	N	P (Pilot) Max	P (Pilot) Min	Q	R	S	W	X	Y	Z (Pilot) Max	Z (Pilot) Min
1	1-1/8	4	3-1/4	3/8	1-7/16	5/16	1-3/4	2-1/4	1.856	2-7/8	4	2.002	2.000	1	2	25/64	3/8	5/8	2-1/4	2.000	1.998
2	1-1/2	4-3/4	3-7/8	15/32	1-3/4	5/16	2-1/4	2-3/4	2.252	3-5/8	6	2.502	2.500	1-1/4	2-1/2	29/64	15/32	11/16	2-3/4	2.500	2.498
3	2	5-3/4	4-3/4	9/16	3-3/16	3/8	2-3/4	3-1/2	2.844	4-5/8	6	3.002	3.000	1-1/2	4	33/64	9/16	3/4	3-1/2	3.000	2.998
4	3	7-1/4	6	5/8	3	3/8	3-1/2	4-1/2	4.500	6-1/2	6	3.752	3.750	2	4	41/64	5/8	15/16	4-1/2	3.750	3.748

aFor intermediate size, see Basic Data in SAE Standard, Marine Propeller-Shaft Ends and Hubs--SAE J755.

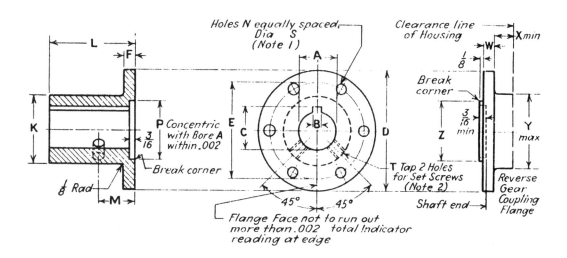

FIG. 2--TYPE I PROPELLER-SHAFT COUPLING, INTERNAL PILOT, STRAIGHT BORE,
SAE FLANGE NO. IS 2S, 3S, and 4S

Note 1--No. 1S flange coupling bolt is to be 3/8--24 X 1-1/4 with plain nut and
lockwasher.
No. 2S flange coupling bolt is to be 7/16--20 X 1-1/2 with plain nut and
lockwasher.
No. 3S flange coupling bolt is to be 1/2--20 X 1-3/4 with plain nut and
lockwasher.
No. 4S flange coupling bolt is to be 5/8--18 X 2 with plain nut and
lockwasher.
Note 2--Either cone or dog point setscrews with spotting of shaft is recommended.
Note 3--See Table 5 for straight bore dimensions A, B, and C.
Note 4--All dimensions are in inches unless otherwise stated (1 in = 25.4 mm).

TABLE 2--PROPELLER-SHAFT COUPLINGS, TYPE I, INTERNAL PILOT--STRAIGHT BORE[a]

SAE Flange No.	Shaft Dia Max	D	E	F	K	L	M	N	S	P (Pilot)		T	W	X	Y	Z (Pilot)	
										Max	Min					Max	Min
1S	1-1/8	4	3-1/4	3/8	2-1/4	2-7/8	1-1/4	4	25/64	2.002	2.000	3/8 - 16	3/8	5/8	2-1/4	2.000	1.998
2S	1-1/2	4-3/4	3-7/8	15/32	2-3/4	3-5/8	1-5/8	6	29/64	2.502	2.500	7/16 - 14	15/32	11/16	2-3/4	2.500	2.498
3S	2	5-3/4	4-3/4	9/16	3-1/2	4-5/8	1-7/8	6	33/64	3.002	3.000	1/2 - 13	9/16	3/4	3-1/2	3.000	2.998
4S	3	7-1/4	6	5/8	4-1/2	6-1/2	2-5/8	6	41/64	3.752	3.750	5/8 - 11	5/8	15/16	4-1/2	3.750	3.748

aFor intermediate size, see Basic Data in SAE Standard, Marine Propeller-Shaft Ends and Hubs--SAE J755.

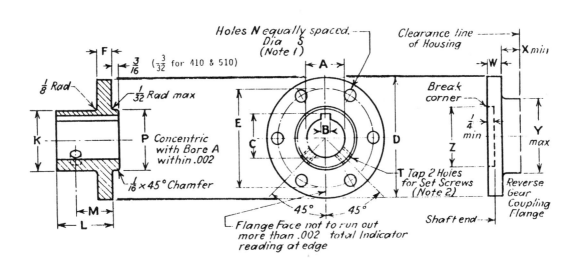

FIG. 3--TYPE II PROPELLER-SHAFT COUPLING, EXTERNAL PILOT, STRAIGHT BORE,
SAE FLANGE NO. 400, 410, 500, 510, 600, AND 725

Note 1--No. 400 flange coupling bolt is to be 3/8--24 X 1-1/2 with plain nut and
lockwasher.
No. 500 flange coupling bolt is to be 7/16--20 X 1-5/8 with plain nut and
lockwasher.
No. 600 flange coupling bolt is to be 1/2--20 X 1-7/8 with plain nut and
lockwasher.
No. 725 flange coupling bolt is to be 5/8--18 X 2-1/4 with plain nut and
lockwasher.
No. 410 and 510 flange coupling bolts to be selected based upon "F" and
"W" flange thickness actually used. Select "X" and "Y" flange dimensions
to clear these fasteners.
Note 2--Either cone or dog point setscrews with spotting of shaft is recommended.
Note 3--See Table 5 for straight bore dimensions A, B, and C.
Note 4--All dimensions are in inches unless otherwise stated (1 in = 25.4 mm;
1 ft = 304.8 mm).

TABLE 3--PROPELLER-SHAFT COUPLINGS, TYPE II, EXTERNAL PILOT--STRAIGHT BORE

SAE Flange No.	Shaft Dia Max	D	E	F	K	L	M	N	S	P (Pilot)		T	W	X	Y	Z (Pilot)	
										Max	Min					Max	Min
400	1-1/4	4	3-1/4	1/2	2	1-7/8	1-1/4	4	25/64	2.000	1.998	3/8 - 16	1/2	5/8	2	2.002	2.000
410	1-1/2	4	3-1/4	5/16 - 3/8	2-1/4	2-5/32	1-9/32	4	25/64	2.499	2.497	3/8 - 16	5/16 - 3/8	Note 1	Note 1	2.501	2.499
500	1-3/4	5	4-1/8	9/16	2-3/4	2-5/8	1-5/8	4	29/64	2.500	2.498	7/16 - 14	9/16	11/16	2-3/4	2.502	2.500
510	2-1/4	5	4-1/4	3/8 - 1/2	3-5/32	2-5/32	1-9/32	4	29/64	2.499	2.497	3/8 - 16	3/8 - 1/2	Note 1	Note 1	2.501	2.499
600	2-1/4	6	5	5/8	3-1/2	3-3/8	1-7/8	6	33/64	3.250	3.248	1/2 - 13	5/8	3/4	3-1/2	3.252	3.250
725	3	7-1/4	6	3/4	4-1/2	4-1/2	2-5/8	6	41/64	4.250	4.248	5/8 - 11	3/4	15/16	4-1/2	4.252	4.250

TABLE 4--TAPER-BORE DIMENSIONS[a], [c]

SAE Flange No.	Nominal Shaft Dia	Bore at A		B		C[b]	
		Min	Max	Min	Max	Min	Max
1	3/4	0.608	0.610	0.1865	0.1875	0.098	0.100
	7/8	0.710	0.712	0.2490	0.2500	0.129	0.131
	1	0.811	0.813	0.2490	0.2500	0.129	0.131
	1-1/8	0.913	0.915	0.2490	0.2500	0.129	0.131
2	1-1/4	1.015	1.017	0.3115	0.3125	0.162	0.165
	1-3/8	1.116	1.118	0.3115	0.3125	0.161	0.164
	1-1/2	1.218	1.220	0.3740	0.3750	0.195	0.198
3	1-3/4	1.421	1.423	0.4365	0.4375	0.226	0.229
	2	1.624	1.626	0.4990	0.5000	0.259	0.262
4	2-1/4	1.827	1.829	0.5610	0.5625	0.291	0.294
	2-1/2	2.030	2.032	0.6235	0.6250	0.322	0.325
	2-3/4	2.233	2.235	0.6235	0.6250	0.322	0.325
	3	2.437	2.439	0.7485	0.7500	0.323	0.326

[a]For intermediate size, see Basic Data in SAE Standard, Marine Propeller-Shaft Ends and Hubs--SAE J755.
[b]Keyway shall be cut parallel to taper.
[c]All dimensions are in inches unless otherwise stated (1 in = 25.4 mm).

TABLE 5--STRAIGHT-BORE DIMENSIONS[a], [c]

SAE FLANGE NUMBERS		Nominal Shaft Dia	A		B[b]		C	
TYPE I	TYPE II		Min	Max	Min	Max	Min	Max
1S	400, 410 & 510	3/4	0.749	0.750	0.1885	0.1905	0.8378	0.8428
1S	400, 410 & 510	7/8	0.874	0.875	0.2510	0.2530	0.9878	0.9928
1S	400, 410 & 510	1	0.999	1.000	0.2510	0.2530	1.1151	1.1201
1S	400, 410 & 510	1-1/8	1.124	1.125	0.2510	0.2530	1.2419	1.2469
2S	400, 410 & 510	1-1/4	1.249	1.250	0.3135	0.3155	1.3924	1.3974
2S	410, 500 & 510	1-3/8	1.374	1.375	0.3135	0.3155	1.5192	1.5242
2S	410, 500 & 510	1-1/2	1.499	1.500	0.3760	0.3780	1.6697	1.6747
	500 & 510	1-5/8	1.624	1.625	0.4385	0.4405	1.8197	1.8247
3S	500 & 510	1-3/4	1.749	1.750	0.4385	0.4405	1.9470	1.9520
	510 & 600	1-7/8	1.874	1.875	0.5010	0.5030	2.0970	2.1020
3S	510 & 600	2	1.999	2.000	0.5010	0.5030	2.2243	2.2293
4S	510 & 600	2-1/4	2.249	2.250	0.5635	0.5655	2.5015	2.5065
4S	725	2-1/2	2.499	2.500	0.6260	0.6280	2.7789	2.7839
4S	725	2-3/4	2.749	2.750	0.6260	0.6280	3.0335	3.0385
4S	725	3	2.999	3.000	0.7510	0.7530	3.3334	3.3384

[a]For intermediate size, see Basic Data in SAE Standard, Marine Propeller-Shaft Ends and Hubs--SAE J755.
[b]Based on Woodruff-key tolerances.
[c]All dimensions are in inches unless otherwise stated (1 in = 25.4 mm).

The phi symbol (∅) is for the convenience of the user in locating areas where technical revisions have been made to the previous issue of the report. If the symbol is next to the report title, it indicates a complete revision of the report.

*Tolerances for SAE Marine Tapers—Surface Finish—*The machined surfaces of propeller hubs and shafting shall be equal to that defined by American Standard B46 as Roughness Symbol 60, which denotes that the root mean square average height of surface irregularities shall not exceed 60 Mu in. (microinches).

*Basic Dimensions—*Taper per foot measured on the diameter and diameter of small end of taper shall be basic dimensions.
Taper Tolerances for Hub Bores
Sizes 3/4 to 1-1/4 in. inclusive, 0.7500 (+0.0000, −0.0020) in. taper per ft.
Sizes 1-3/8 to 2 in. inclusive, 0.7500 (+0.0000, −0.0019) in. taper per ft.

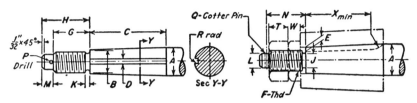

TAPER = 3/4 IN. ON DIAMETER PER FT = 1/16 IN. PER IN. = 3 DEG 34 MIN 47 SEC TOTAL INCLUDED ANGLE

FIG. 1—PROPELLER-SHAFT ENDS

TABLE 1—DIMENSIONS FOR SHAFTS FROM 3/4 TO 3 IN. IN DIAMETER

Nominal Shaft Dia, A	Dia Small End, B Min	Dia Small End, B Max	Taper Length, C	Keyway Width, D Nominal	Keyway Width, D Min	Keyway Width, D Max	Keyway Side Depth,[a] Nominal	Keyway Side Depth,[a] Min	Keyway Side Depth,[a] Max	Keyway Fillet Radius,[b] R	Thread,[c] F Dia	Thread,[c] F Threads per in.	End of Taper to End of Thread, G	Extension Beyond Taper, H
3/4	0.624	0.626	2	3/16	0.1865	0.1875	3/32	0.095	0.097	1/32	1/2	13	1-1/16	1-5/16
7/8	0.726	0.728	2-3/8	1/4	0.249	0.250	1/8	0.125	0.127	1/32	5/8	11	1-1/4	1-1/2
1	0.827	0.829	2-3/4	1/4	0.249	0.250	1/8	0.125	0.127	1/32	3/4	10	1-7/16	1-3/4
1-1/8	0.929	0.931	3-1/8	1/4	0.249	0.250	1/8	0.125	0.127	1/32	3/4	10	1-7/16	1-3/4
1-1/4	1.030	1.032	3-1/2	5/16	0.3115	0.3125	5/32	0.157	0.160	1/16	7/8	9	1-5/8	2
1-3/8	1.132	1.134	3-7/8	5/16	0.3115	0.3125	5/32	0.157	0.160	1/16	1	8	1-13/16	2-1/4
1-1/2	1.233	1.235	4-1/4	3/8	0.374	0.375	3/16	0.189	0.192	1/16	1-1/8	7	2	2-7/16
1-3/4	1.437	1.439	5	7/16	0.4365	0.4375	7/32	0.219	0.222	1/16	1-1/4	7	2-1/4	2-3/4
2	1.640	1.642	5-3/4	1/2	0.499	0.500	1/4	0.251	0.254	1/16	1-1/2	6	2-5/8	3-1/8
2-1/4	1.843	1.845	6-1/2	9/16	0.561	0.5625	9/32	0.281	0.284	3/32	1-3/4	5	3	3-1/2
2-1/2	2.046	2.048	7-1/4	5/8	0.6235	0.625	5/16	0.315	0.312	3/32	1-3/4	5	3	3-1/2
2-3/4	2.257	2.259	7-7/8	5/8	0.6235	0.625	5/16	0.313	0.316	3/32	2	4-1/2	3-1/2	4
3	2.460	2.462	8-5/8	3/4	0.7485	0.750	5/16	0.311	0.314	3/32	2-1/4	4-1/2	3-7/8	4-3/8

TABLE 1—DIMENSIONS FOR SHAFTS FROM 3/4 TO 3 IN. IN DIAMETER (CONTINUED)

Nominal Shaft Dia, A	Undercut J	Undercut K	Dia of Pin End, L	Length of Pin End, M	Cotter Pin Hole N	Cotter Pin Hole P (Drill)	Cotter Pin, Q Nominal Dia	Cotter Pin, Q Length	Nuts[d] Size	Nuts[d] Plain Thickness, T	Nuts[d] Jam Thickness, W	Keyway Length, X
3/4	25/64	1/8	3/8	1/4	1-9/64	9/64	1/8	3/4	1/2—13	1/2	5/16	1-1/2
7/8	31/64	1/8	7/16	1/4	1-21/64	9/64	1/8	3/4	5/8—11	5/8	3/8	1-25/32
1	19/32	1/8	1/2	5/16	1-33/64	9/64	1/8	1	3/4—10	3/4	7/16	2-1/8
1-1/8	19/32	1/8	1/2	5/16	1-33/64	9/64	1/8	1	3/4—10	3/4	7/16	2-1/8
1-1/4	23/32	1/8	5/8	3/8	1-23/32	11/64	5/32	1-1/4	7/8—9	7/8	1/2	2-13/16
1-3/8	13/16	1/8	3/4	7/16	1-29/32	11/64	5/32	1-1/2	1 —8	1	9/16	3-3/16
1-1/2	29/32	3/16	7/8	7/16	2-3/32	11/64	5/32	1-1/2	1-1/8—9	1-1/8	5/8	3-1/2
1-3/4	1-1/32	3/16	1	1/2	2-23/64	13/64	3/16	1-3/4	1-1/4—7	1-1/4	3/4	4-7/32
2	1-1/4	3/16	1-1/4	1/2	2-47/64	13/64	3/16	2	1-1/2—6	1-1/2	7/8	4-15/16
2-1/4	1-3/8	3/16	1-3/8	1/2	3-9/64	17/64	1/4	2-1/4	1-3/4—5	1-3/4	1	5-5/8
2-1/2	1-7/16	3/16	1-7/16	1/2	3-9/64	17/64	1/4	2-1/4	1-3/4—5	1-3/4	1	6-3/32
2-3/4	1-11/16	1/4	1-11/16	1/2	3-41/64	17/64	1/4	2-1/2	2 —4-1/2	2	1-1/8	6-21/32
3	1-15/16	1/4	1-15/16	1/2	4-1/64	17/64	1/4	3	2-1/4—4-1/2	2-1/4	1-1/4	7-11/32

[a] Keyway shall be cut parallel to taper.
[b] Fillets are recommended for keyways in shafts through 2 in. in diameter. Fillets are mandatory for shafts above 2 in. in diameter.
[c] Threads are Unified and American Standard, Class 3A.
[d] Nuts are to be semifinished stock, American Standard B18.2

Sizes 2-1/4 to 3 in. inclusive, 0.7500 (+0.0000, −0.0015) in. taper per ft.
Sizes 3-1/4 to 5-1/2 in. inclusive, 0.7500 (+0.0000, −0.0013) in. taper per ft.
Sizes 6 to 8 in. inclusive, 1.0000 (+0.0000, −0.0013) in. taper per ft.
Taper Tolerances for Shafts
Sizes 3/4 to 1-1/4 in. inclusive, 0.7500 (+0.0020, −0.0000) in. taper per ft.
Sizes 1-3/8 to 2 in. inclusive, 0.7500 (+0.0019, −0.0000) in. taper per ft.
Sizes 2-1/4 to 3 in. inclusive, 0.7500 (+0.0015, −0.0000) in. taper per ft.
Sizes 3-1/4 to 5-1/2 in. inclusive, 0.7500 (+0.0013, −0.0000) in. taper per ft.
Sizes 6 to 8 in. inclusive, 1.0000 (+0.0013, −0.0000) in. taper per ft.
*Basic Data—Keyways—*The keyway shall be cut parallel to taper. At the small end of the hub length and shaft taper length, the keyway shall have the specified side depth. The keyway side depth shall be measured normal to the axis of the taper, not normal to the surface of the taper.

*Keys—*Keys for use in filleted keyways must be chamfered so that the corners of the key do not touch the keyway fillets.
Small-End Diameter of Taper for Hubs—For nominal bore diameters 3-1/4 to 4 in. inclusive, the small end of the taper shall be 0.8125 times the nominal bore diameter.
For nominal bore diameters 4-1/2 to 5-1/2 in. inclusive, the small end of the taper shall be 0.84375 times the nominal bore diameter.
For nominal bore diameters 6 to 8 in. inclusive, the small end of the taper shall be 0.79167 times the nominal bore diameter.
Small-End Diameter of Taper for Shafts—For nominal shaft diameters 3/4 to 2-1/2 in. inclusive, the small end of the taper shall be 0.8125 times the nominal shaft diameter plus 0.01562 in.

For nominal shaft diameters $2\frac{3}{4}$ to 4 in. inclusive, the small end of the taper shall be 0.8125 times the nominal shaft diameter plus 0.02344 in.

For nominal shaft diameters $4\frac{1}{2}$ to $5\frac{1}{2}$ in. inclusive, the small end of the taper shall be 0.84375 times the nominal shaft diameter plus 0.03125 in.

For nominal shaft diameters 6 to 8 in. inclusive, the small end of the taper shall be 0.79167 times the nominal shaft diameter plus 0.04167 in.

Intermediate-Size Tapers—The required small-end taper diameter of hub bore and shaft end for intermediate diameters not covered by this Standard shall be calculated from data given above using the next smaller standard taper data.

The keyway for intermediate-size hub bore and shaft end shall be that specified for the next smallest standard bore and shaft.

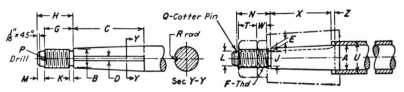

TAPER OF SHAFTS TO 6 IN. DIAMETER = 3/4 IN. ON DIAMETER PER FT = 1/16 IN. PER IN. = 3 DEG 34 MIN 47 SEC TOTAL INCLUDED ANGLE
TAPER OF SHAFTS 6 IN. AND LARGER = 1 IN. ON DIAMETER PER FT = 1/12 IN. PER IN. = 4 DEG 46 MIN 19 SEC TOTAL INCLUDED ANGLE

FIG. 2—PROPELLER-SHAFT ENDS

TABLE 2—DIMENSIONS FOR SHAFTS FROM 3-1/4 TO 8 IN. IN DIAMETER[a]

Nominal Shaft Dia, A	Dia Small End, B Min	Dia Small End, B Max	Taper Length, C	Keyway Width, D Nominal	Keyway Width, D Min	Keyway Width, D Max	Keyway Side Depth,[b] E Nominal	Keyway Side Depth,[b] E Min	Keyway Side Depth,[b] E Max	Keyway Fillet Radius, R	Thread,[c] F Dia	Thread,[c] F Threads per in.	End of Taper to End of Thread, G	Extension Beyond Taper, H
3-1/4	2.663	2.665	9-3/8	3/4	0.7485	0.750	5/16	0.311	0.314	1/8	2-1/2	4	4-3/8	5-1/8
3-1/2	2.866	2.868	10-1/8	7/8	0.8735	0.875	5/16	0.310	0.313	1/8	2-1/2	4	4-3/8	5-1/8
3-3/4	3.069	3.071	10-7/8	7/8	0.8735	0.875	5/16	0.310	0.313	1/8	2-3/4	4	4-3/4	5-1/2
4	3.272	3.274	11-5/8	1	0.9985	1.000	5/16	0.309	0.312	1/8	3	4	5-1/8	5-7/8
4-1/2	3.827	3.829	10-3/4	1-1/8	1.123	1.125	3/8	0.373	0.376	5/32	3-1/4	4	5-5/8	6-3/8
5	4.249	4.251	12	1-1/4	1.248	1.250	7/16	0.434	0.437	3/16	3-3/4	4	6-3/8	7-1/8
5-1/2	4.671	4.673	13-1/4	1-1/4	1.248	1.250	7/16	0.435	0.438	3/16	4	4	6-3/4	7-3/8
6	4.791	4.793	14-1/2	1-3/8	1.373	1.375	1/2	0.493	0.496	7/32	4-1/4	4	7-1/2	8-1/2
6-1/2	5.187	5.189	15-3/4	1-3/8	1.373	1.375	1/2	0.494	0.497	7/32	4-1/4	4	8-1/4	9-1/4
7	5.582	5.584	17	1-1/2	1.498	1.500	9/16	0.555	0.558	1/4	5	4	9	10
7-1/2	5.978	5.980	18-1/4	1-1/2	1.498	1.500	9/16	0.556	0.559	1/4	5-1/2	4	9-3/8	10-3/8
8	6.374	6.376	19-1/2	1-3/4	1.748	1.750	9/16	0.553	0.556	1/4	5-3/4	4	9-3/4	10-3/4

TABLE 2—DIMENSIONS FOR SHAFTS FROM 3-1/4 TO 8 IN. IN DIAMETER[a] (CONTINUED)

Nominal Shaft Dia, A	Undercut J	Undercut K	Dia of Pin End, L	Length of Pin End, M	Cotter Pin Hole N	Cotter Pin Hole P (Drill)	Cotter Pin, Q Nominal Dia	Cotter Pin, Q Length	Nuts[d] Size	Nuts[d] Plain Thickness, T	Nuts[d] Jam Thickness, W	Sleeve Dia,[e] U Min	Sleeve Dia,[e] U Max	Clearance, Z	Keyway, X
3-1/4	2-1/8	3/8	2-1/8	3/4	4-37/64	3/8	3/8	3	2-1/2—4	2-1/2	1-1/2	3.870	3.872	3/8	8-1/2
3-1/2	2-1/8	3/8	2-1/8	3/4	4-37/64	3/8	3/8	3	2-1/2—4	2-1/2	1-1/2	4.120	4.122	3/8	9-1/4
3-3/4	2-3/8	3/8	2-3/8	3/4	4-61/64	3/8	3/8	3-1/2	2-3/4—4	2-3/4	1-5/8	4.369	4.371	3/8	10
4	2-1/2	3/8	2-1/2	3/4	5-21/64	3/8	3/8	3-1/2	3 —4	3	1-3/4	4.619	4.621	3/8	10-1/2
4-1/2	2-3/4	3/8	2-3/4	3/4	—	—	—	—	3-1/4—4	3-1/4	1-7/8	5.243	5.245	1/2	9-5/8
5	3-1/4	3/8	3-1/4	3/4	—	—	—	—	3-3/4—4	3-3/4	2-1/8	5.993	5.995	1/2	10-7/8
5-1/2	3-1/2	1/2	3-1/2	1	—	—	—	—	4 —4	4	2-1/4	6.492	6.494	1/2	12-1/8
6	3-7/8	1/2	3-7/8	1	—	—	—	—	4-1/4—4	4-1/4	2-1/4	6.992	6.994	1/2	13-1/4
6-1/2	4-3/8	1/2	4-3/8	1	—	—	—	—	4-1/2—4	4-1/2	2-1/2	7.492	7.494	1/2	14-3/8
7	4-7/8	1/2	4-7/8	1	—	—	—	—	5 —4	5	2-3/4	8.117	8.120	1/2	15-5/8
7-1/2	5-1/8	1/2	5-1/8	1	—	—	—	—	5-1/2—4	5-1/2	3	8.616	8.619	1/2	16-7/8
8	5-3/8	1/2	5-3/8	1	—	—	—	—	5-3/4—4	5-3/4	3-1/8	9.240	9.243	1/2	18-1/8

[a] A steel shaft may be used in salt water if a suitable aft Fairwater is used.
[b] Keyway shall be cut parallel to taper.
[c] Threads are Unified and American Standard, Class 3A.
[d] Nuts are to be semifinished stock, American Standard B18.2.
[e] The shaft sleeve shown is recommended practice, but the use of a sleeve is optional.

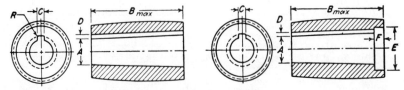

TAPER = 3/4 IN. ON DIAMETER PER FT = 1/16 IN. PER IN. = 3 DEG 34 MIN 47 SEC TOTAL INCLUDED ANGLE

FIG. 3—PROPELLER HUBS

Shaft Taper and Coupling Dimensions

TABLE 3—HUBS FOR SHAFTS FROM 3/4 TO 3 IN. IN DIAMETER, INCLUSIVE, WITHOUT SLEEVE [a]

Nominal Bore Dia	Dia Small End, A Min	Dia Small End, A Max	Length, B	Keyway Width, C Nominal	Keyway Width, C Min	Keyway Width, C Max	Keyway Side Depth, D [b] Nominal	Keyway Side Depth, D Min	Keyway Side Depth, D Max	Keyway Fillet Radius, R [c]
3/4	0.608	0.610	2-1/4	3/16	0.1865	0.1875	3/32	0.098	0.100	1/32
7/8	0.710	0.712	2-5/8	1/4	0.249	0.250	1/8	0.129	0.131	1/32
1	0.811	0.813	3	1/4	0.249	0.250	1/8	0.129	0.131	1/32
1-1/8	0.913	0.915	3-3/8	1/4	0.249	0.250	1/8	0.129	0.131	1/32
1-1/4	1.015	1.017	3-3/4	5/16	0.3115	0.3125	5/32	0.162	0.165	1/16
1-3/8	1.116	1.118	4-1/8	5/16	0.3115	0.3125	5/32	0.161	0.164	1/16
1-1/2	1.218	1.220	4-1/2	3/8	0.374	0.375	3/16	0.195	0.198	1/16
1-3/4	1.421	1.423	5-1/4	7/16	0.4365	0.4375	7/32	0.226	0.229	1/16
2	1.624	1.626	6	1/2	0.499	0.500	1/4	0.259	0.262	1/16
2-1/4	1.827	1.829	6-3/4	9/16	0.561	0.5625	9/32	0.291	0.294	3/32
2-1/2	2.030	2.032	7-1/2	5/8	0.6235	0.625	5/16	0.322	0.325	3/32
2-3/4	2.233	2.235	8-1/4	5/8	0.6235	0.625	5/16	0.322	0.325	3/32
3	2.437	2.439	9	3/4	0.7485	0.750	5/16	0.323	0.326	3/32

[a] For intermediate sizes and other design data, see Basic Data.
[b] Keyway shall be cut parallel to taper. Keyway side depth is measured normal to axis of taper.
[c] Fillets are recommended for keyways in hubs for shafts through 2 in. in diameter. Fillets are mandatory in hubs for shafts above 2 in. in diameter.

TABLE 4—HUBS FOR SHAFTS FROM 3-1/4 TO 8 IN. IN DIAMETER [a]

Nominal Bore Dia [b]	Shafts Without Sleeve Dia Small End, A Min	A Max	Length, B	Keyway Width, C Nominal	Min	Max	Keyway Side Depth, D Nominal	Min	Max	Keyway Fillet Radius, R	Shafts with Sleeve Dia, E [c] Min	Max	Depth, F
3-1/4	2.640	2.642	9-3/4	3/4	0.7485	0.750	5/16	0.323	0.326	1/8	3.875	3.878	7/8
3-1/2	2.843	2.845	10-1/2	7/8	0.8735	0.875	5/16	0.324	0.327	1/8	4.125	4.128	7/8
3-3/4	3.046	3.048	11-1/4	7/8	0.8735	0.875	5/16	0.324	0.327	1/8	4.375	4.378	7/8
4	3.249	3.251	12	1	0.9985	1.000	5/16	0.326	0.329	1/8	4.625	4.628	1-1/8
4-1/2	3.796	3.798	11-1/4	1-1/8	1.123	1.125	3/8	0.388	0.391	5/32	5.250	5.253	1-1/8
5	4.218	4.220	12-1/2	1-1/4	1.248	1.250	7/16	0.450	0.453	3/16	6.000	6.003	1-1/8
5-1/2	4.640	4.642	13-3/4	1-1/4	1.248	1.250	7/16	0.450	0.453	3/16	6.500	6.503	1-1/4
6	4.749	4.751	15	1-3/8	1.373	1.375	1/2	0.517	0.520	7/32	7.000	7.003	1-1/4
6-1/2	5.145	5.147	16-1/4	1-3/8	1.373	1.375	1/2	0.516	0.519	7/32	7.500	7.503	1-3/8
7	5.541	5.543	17-1/2	1-1/2	1.498	1.500	9/16	0.579	0.582	1/4	8.125	8.128	1-3/8
7-1/2	5.937	5.939	18-3/4	1-1/2	1.498	1.500	9/16	0.579	0.582	1/4	8.625	8.628	1-3/8
8	6.332	6.334	20	1-3/4	1.748	1.750	9/16	0.582	0.585	1/4	9.250	9.253	1-3/8

[a] For intermediate sizes and other design data, see Basic Data.
[b] On hubs for shafts 6 in. and larger, taper is 1 in. on diameter per ft, equals 1/12 in. per in., equals 4 deg 46 minutes 19 sec total included angle.
[c] The use of a shaft sleeve is recommended for shafts 3-1/4 in. in diameter and over. The propeller-hub counterbore is to be used only with shafts having the sleeve.

Appendix D
Decimal Exponents

Throughout this book extensive use is made of decimal exponents. For instance, in Formula 5-2 [**SLIP = 1.4 ÷ Kts$^{0.57}$**], 0.57 is the decimal exponent.

To solve this on a scientific calculator is as simple as entering the value for knots, pressing the exponentiation key, and entering the exponent of 0.57. This will give the value for Kts$^{0.57}$ quickly and easily.

For those not familiar with decimal exponents, however, it is a good idea to understand what they are:

$X^{0.5}$ is the same as $X^{1/2}$ is the same as $\sqrt{X}$ or $\sqrt[2]{X}$, the square root of X;

$X^{0.334}$ is the same as $X^{1/3}$ is the same as $\sqrt[3]{X}$, the cube root of X;

and so on.

You can see that a decimal is just another way of writing a fraction and that it makes no difference whether we use a decimal or a fraction as the exponent. (The decimal, of course, is the easiest to enter in a calculator.)

You can also see that a decimal or fractional exponent is the same as taking the root of a number, and that the root is always the same as the inverse of the decimal. Thus, raising a number to the 0.5 power is the same as taking the square root of that number. (The inverse of $0.5 = 1 \div 0.5 = 2$, and $\sqrt{x}$ is the same as $\sqrt[2]{x}$.) Raising a number to the 0.334 power is the same as taking the cube root of that number. (The inverse of $0.334 = 1 \div 0.334 = 3$, giving $\sqrt[3]{x}$.)

The nice thing about decimal exponents is that they allow quick manipulation of formulas with exponential relationships that do not happen to fall exactly on even powers or roots such as square and cube roots. In the case of Formula 5–2, the data showed that slip did not vary exactly as the square root of speed in knots, but as speed to the 0.57 power. This relationship could be rewritten a number of ways:

Kts$^{0.57}$ is the same as Kts$^{57/100}$ is the same as $\sqrt[100]{Kts^{57}}$

Not only is the 0.57 exponent easier to enter into a calculator, it's easier to write as well. As an example, if we were to raise 12 knots to the 0.57 power, the answer would be 4.121, while 25 knots raised to the 0.57 power would equal 6.264.

Manufacturers and Suppliers

Arneson Marine, Inc. 15 Koch Road, Unit E, Corte Madera, CA 94925–surface propellers for high-speed craft

Bird-Johnson Company, 110 Norfolk Street, Walpole, MA 02081–fixed- and controllable-pitch propellers for commercial applications

Brunton's Propellers Ltd, Station Road, Sudbury, Suffolk CO10 6ST England

Caterpillar Inc., Engine Division Market Development, 100 N.E. Adams Street, Peoria, IL 61629

Escher Wyss Propellers, Sulzer-Escher Wyss, GmbH, D-7980 Ravensburg, F.R.G.–hydraulically operated, controllable-pitch propellers for commercial applications

Hollming Ltd., PO Box 14 26101 Rauma, Finland–Aquamaster steerable Z-drive units

Hundested Motor & Propeller Fabrik A/S, Skansevij 1, DK-3390, Hundested, Denmark–controllable-pitch propellers

Jatstram Ltd., 219 E. 6th Street, North Vancouver, BC, Canada V7L 1P4–geared folding propellers for sailboats

Kaama Marine Engineering, Inc., 936 Sunset Drive, Costa Mesa, CA 92627–surface propellers for high-speed craft

Kahlenberg Bros. Co., PO Box 358, Two Rivers, WI 54241–fixed-pitch propellers for yacht and commercial applications

KaMeWa, Kristinehamm Works, S-68101 Kristinehamm, Sweden—controllable-pitch propellers for large, fast yachts, patrol boats and commercial applications

Kiekhaefer Aeromarine, Inc., 1970 Aeromarine Dr., Fond du Lac, WI 54935–propellers for high-speed pleasure and racing craft, outboard, sterndrive and inboard

Laird Engineering, 3705 West Carmel, Peoria, IL 61615

Liaaen Helix a/s, Godoygt. 8, N-6000 Aalesund,Norway—controllable-pitch propellers for commercial applications

Lipps BV, PO Box 6, 5150 BB Drunen, The Netherlands–propellers for commercial applications

Mercury Marine, Fond du Lac, WI 54935–propellers for outboards and sterndrives

Michigan Wheel Corporation, 1501 Buchanan Ave., SW, Grand Rapids, MI 49507–fixed-pitch propellers for all yacht and commercial applications, ducted propeller systems

PVI Inc., PO Box 71098, Seattle WA 98107–geared feathering propellers for sailboats

Schottle (UK) Ltd. 4 Paradise Row, Bethnal Green, London E2 9LE, England–steerable Z-drives

Scandinavian Propellers Ltd., 22–26 Industriskellet DK-3300, Frederiksvaerk, Denmark–controllable-pitch propellers

Vetus UK Ltd, Greasley Street, Bulwell, Nottingham, Notts NG6 8NJ England

W.H. Denouden (USA) Inc., PO Box 8712, Baltimore, MD 21240–propellers for small craft and sailing yachts

Bibliography

Arneson Surface Drives: Basic Considerations for Designers and Builders, by Douglas E. Railton and Paul Kamen, Arneson Marine, Inc. Corte Madera, CA (paper presented at 1988 Westlawn Yacht Design Symposium)

Basic Naval Architecture, 3rd Edition, by Kenneth C. Barnaby, Hutchinson Scientific and Technical, London, England, 1960

Basic Ship Theory, Vols. I & II, by K. J. Rawson and E. C. Tupper, Longman Scientific & Technical, Essex, England, 1983

Caldwell's Screw Tug Design, by A. Caldwell, revised by Jeffrey N. Wood, A. S. Barnes and Company, Inc. Cranbury, NJ, 1970

Elements of Yacht Design, by Norman L. Skene, Kennedy Bros. Inc., New York, NY 1938 (modern edition appears later in this list)

High Speed Small Craft, 4th Edition, by Peter du Cane, John de Graff, Inc., Tuckahoe, NY, 1973

How Fast Will It Go? Performance Limits of High Speed Planing Hulls, by Morley S. Smith, The Planimeter, Volume 36, Winter, No.2, the Society of Small Craft Designers

Mark's Standard Handbook for Mechanical Engineers, 8th Edition, Theodore Baumeister, Editor-in-Chief, McGraw Hill Book Company, New York, NY, 1978

Metal Corrosion in Boats, by Nigel Warren, International Marine, Camden, ME, and Adlard Coles Ltd., London, 1980

Motor Yacht and Boat Design, by Douglas Phillips-Birt, Adlard Coles Limited, London, England, 1966

Naval Architecture of Planing Hulls, 3rd Edition, by Lindsay Lord, Cornell Maritime Press, Cambridge MD, 1963

Primer of Towing, by George H. Reid, Cornell Maritime Press, Cambridge, MD, 1975

Propeller Selection, by Kevin Mitchell & Robert Kress (paper presented at 1983 Westlawn Yacht Design Symposium)

Safety Standards for Small Craft, American Boat & Yacht Council, Millersville, MD, last update 1988

Skene's Elements of Yacht Design, 18th Edition, by Francis S. Kinney, Dodd, Mead, New York, NY, 1973

Theory and Practice of Propellers for Auxiliary Sailboats, by John R. Stanton, Cornell Maritime Press, Cambridge, MD, 1975

Tugs, Towboats and Towing, by Edward M. Brady, Cornell Maritime Press, Cambridge, MD, 1974

Voyaging Under Power, by Robert P. Beebe, International Marine/Seven Seas Press, Camden, ME, 1975

Index